Growing Together

Growing Together

JOHN T. TRENT

VICTOR

BOOKS a division of SP Publications, Inc.
WHEATON, ILLINOIS 60187

Offices also in
Whitby, Ontario, Canada
Amersham-on-the-Hill, Bucks, England

All names used in this book have been changed to ensure my counselees' confidentiality.

All Scripture quotations are from the *New American Standard Bible*, © 1960, 1962, 1968, 1971, 1972, 1973, 1975 by The Lockman Foundation, La Habra, California.

Recommended Dewey Decimal Classification: 173
Suggested Subject Heading: MARRIAGE

Library of Congress Catalog Card Number: 84-52367
ISBN: 0-89693-323-7

VICTOR BOOKS
A division of SP Publications, Inc.
Wheaton, Illinois 60187

Contents

Acknowledgments

I would like to express my deepest thanks and appreciation to the following people who contributed in large measure to this book becoming a reality.

- To Dr. Howard Hendricks, who first opened my eyes to the way the Scriptures can enrich a marriage.

- To Drs. Meier, Minirth, Wichern, and Kershaw, for their patience in teaching me practical counseling skills.

- To Dr. Michael Burnidge, for his supportive friendship and invaluable help in organizing the original outline of this book.

- To Mr. David Bourne, my editor at Victor Books, for his help and hard work in revising this manuscript.

- To Pastors Jim Rose and Darryl DelHousaye, and the associate pastors, elders, and body of believers at Northwest Bible Church, Dallas, Texas and Scottsdale Bible Church, Scottsdale, Arizona. These two Christ-centered churches provided me with living models of married couples committed to growing together.

*This book is dedicated
to my loving wife, Cynthia,
who enriches my life
and teaches me daily lessons
on growing in marriage and ministry*

ONE

Falling Apart or Growing Together?

We live in a culture that loves to watch things fall apart. Recently, in the city where my wife and I live, several hundred persons stood around for hours to watch the demolition of an old high-rise building. When that once mighty structure began to rumble, then shake, and finally crumble to the ground, a huge roar rose from the crowd.

As a pastor and counselor, I've noticed that buildings aren't the only things crashing down these days. With alarming frequency, the marital structures of many couples are being jolted and destroyed. Every week in my office, I see couples exchange pledges of undying love for bitter accusations and shattered dreams. In a day and age when the prevailing attitude toward marriage seems to be, "when the going gets tough, get another partner," one wonders if there is any hope for couples who still believe in marital commitment.

Without a doubt, I believe there is. The purpose of this book, in fact, is to present a biblically based marriage enrichment program that can help couples learn to "grow together" in the various aspects of their relationship. By relying on God's wisdom and Word for instruction, hope *does* exist for couples who are convinced that divorce is not the answer to their problems.

But just what do the words "marriage enrichment" mean? And does this book really have anything to say to couples who feel their marriage *already* is in good shape? After all, aren't these marriage manuals only for people with *problems?* These are both relevant questions; both deserve answers.

First, marriage enrichment involves the process of developing, nurturing, and improving one's marriage relationship; because this relationship is multidimensional, enrichment can be directed toward any number of different marital needs: emotional, spiritual, intellectual. The specific techniques of this nurturing process will, of course, be explored throughout this book.

Second, marriage enrichment isn't only for couples who have serious problems to work through. On the contrary, it's designed to enhance relationships *before* they fall into disarray. Occasionally, a couple will come in for counseling who already have a "growing" marriage. I believe such couples are a step ahead of the game. Why? Because they haven't waited for their relationship to deteriorate before seeking encouragement and help. They've taken steps to enrich and protect a healthy relationship through "preventive action" *before* permanent damage is done. If more couples followed this practice, I'm convinced many marriages could be saved before they reach a critical phase.

This principle of "preventive action" is one that Solomon, himself, recognized as beneficial and helpful. After viewing a field where neglect had destroyed a potentially rich harvest, he observed:

"A little sleep, a little slumber,
A little folding of the hands to rest,"
Then your poverty will come as a robber,
And your want like an armed man
(Prov. 24:33-34).

Solomon realized that the owner of this field had failed to tend it. Had the farmer worked to restore his property *before* it fell into disrepair, the crop might have been saved.

For couples, neglect of one's marriage can produce the same devastating results. Just as a field cannot yield crops without careful cultivation, a marriage cannot produce true joy without dedication, compassion, and a desire to more fully understand one's spouse. This is where a biblical marriage enrichment program can provide timely help.

But how is the enrichment program outlined in this book any different from those presented in similar guides? How can this particular plan help couples awake from the stupifying sleep into which society has lured them?

Basically, after several years of counseling couples and performing extensive research on the subject of marriage enrichment, I've found that a successful marriage enrichment program must be based on at least four principles—all of which are foundational to the program presented in these pages.

First, a marriage enrichment program must do more than simply show couples how to dissect their marital problems. It must go beyond merely breaking problems down to their constituent parts. It must explain how relationships can be improved and rebuilt.

As a young boy, I once spent a Thanksgiving at the home of my uncle, a surgeon. When it came time to carve the turkey, I grabbed a knife and begged for the job. Graciously, my uncle allowed me to carve the bird and I did so with what I thought was particular care and skill.

"There," I said, barely masking my pride, "I could be a surgeon too, don't you think?"

In his wise manner, my uncle paused, then said, "John, you've shown us you can cut. Now let's see how you are at putting it back together again!"

The problem with some marriage enrichment programs I've seen is similar to the one I faced after carving the turkey. These programs do a beautiful job of showing a couple how to carve up their marriage and inspect each slice, but fail to help them put their relationship back together. An enrichment program must be able to explain how relationships can be reassembled once they have been critically examined.

Second, this type of program needs to focus on the concerns of *both* persons in the marriage relationship. Many marriage manuals seem designed solely to help the reader identify his or her *own* strengths and weaknesses. Yet where marriage is concerned, insight into just one person's character usually is not sufficient to bring about needed change. We need to study our spouse as well as ourselves. Only then will we be able to understand the interactions which occur between two distinct personalities. This, in itself, is a major step toward achieving marital "oneness."

Third, we must acknowledge that a marriage enrichment program is meant to change us. In even the best of marriages, the potential for further growth always is present.

Walt Disney was a person who understood the dynamics of constant growth. He never was content to rest on the laurels of his past achievements. One of his longtime co-workers has explained that while Disney was alive, he allowed many of his competitors to examine the behind-the-scenes workings of rides and attractions at Disneyland.

When asked why he permitted his competition to view his "secrets," Disney replied, "If we are doing our job properly, by the time someone imitates our attraction, we'll already have created a new and better one."

What an attitude! His desire to stay on the cutting edge of innovation left a legacy that now includes Disney World and the EPCOT Center. This determination to remain creative and open to change is the same kind of attitude couples need to possess to grow closer together.

Finally, as mentioned earlier, we need to recognize the role God plays as the cornerstone of the marriage enrichment process. The Apostle Paul speaks of a source of strength that can move a couple out of the deepest marital rut: "If any man is in Christ, he is a new creature; the old things [have] passed away; behold, new things have come" (2 Cor. 5:17). The potential for change is present in anyone who has a personal relationship with Jesus Christ. In His strength is the power to change even the oldest or most frustrating pattern of behavior.

Explaining how relationships can be enriched and rebuilt; learning about the concerns of both husband and wife; being open to new challenges and change; keeping Christ as our cornerstone—these are challenging principles. But if they're to produce growth, insight, and change in our marriage, we'll first need to find some realistic and practical means to apply them, means that can result in growth, insight, change, and a deeper understanding of one's marriage.

Therefore, for those who would like to get the most out of this enrichment program, here are a few helpful suggestions.

First, plan to study this material together. Marriage is a team sport. While you *can* gain certain skills by practicing alone, working with your spouse will help you make even greater progress. With all the opportunities our society provides for us to be "independent" of one another, why not make the reading of this book a special joint project?

Second, try to work through this book in the order in which it is written. Some chapters may look more "interesting" or seem to be "just what I need." However, the material is presented in stair-step fashion; climbing is best done one step at a time. In fact, in some cases, the material that seems least appealing will deal with issues you most need to consider.

Third, complete the follow-up questions found at the end of each chapter. The questions and activities listed there can help move concepts off the page and into real life settings.

In sum, if you have read every marital self-help book on the market, try reading this book in a different way. Rather than using it to find support for your way of doing things, or to discover labels for your spouse's problems, make a daily effort to adopt some of the suggestions outlined in this book. Relating to one another in new and different ways can open up rich avenues in your relationship.

Christian couples have a clear choice. They either can flirt with a world that attacks commitment and marriage, or, by following biblical guidelines, they can begin to build up a lasting love and marriage. My prayer is that you will find these pages to be not just another academic exercise, but a personally enriching experience. Are you ready to begin? I hope so. A world of opportunities awaits those committed to *growing together.*

TWO

How Firm a Foundation?

I spend a fair amount of time visiting people who, for one reason or another, are in the hospital. As a pastor, this task is part of my job—and it's not without certain rewards. For example, I've come away from a number of these brief visits with some rather interesting insights into the human condition. For reasons I've yet to fully understand, the stark reality of hospital life seems to expose many individuals' true beliefs and values. Such was the case with two men I visited on the same day in a large, metropolitan hospital.

I stepped off the elevator at the fourth floor and made my way to the room of a man who was an infrequent attender at our church. As far as I knew, he was not a believer. Regrettably, the few minutes I spent with him were tense and uncomfortable. He was scheduled to undergo major surgery in a few days, was extremely bitter over being ill, and was making life miserable for his poor wife and for every nurse on the hall.

After several unsuccessful attempts at conversation, I finally asked him if we could pray together. "Why should I pray?" he snapped. "It won't keep me from having this operation, will it?" The harshness of his voice left me momentarily speechless.

Fortunately, his wife intervened and thanked me for coming by. But her husband's eyes shot me an all-too-clear message: my one visit was more than enough, thank you. I left the room feeling frustrated and saddened.

By now, I was ready to turn in my chaplain's badge and go home. But grudgingly, I walked to the elevator and headed up two floors to check in on another one of our members.

He was seventy years old, dying of cancer. I had planned to offer a few words of hope and comfort, then depart. But it was not to be; after a few minutes with this man, I realized the tables had been turned. I found that rather than ministering to *him*, he was ministering to *me*. I listened in awe as this godly saint spoke of life's blessings and difficulties, but without regret. His wife of over forty years was with him; she shared his bold confidence that soon he would be "seeing the Saviour." Our visit ended when he took *my* hand and suggested we pray.

I had traveled only two floors, but I had seen men who were worlds apart. The foundation of the first man's life had cracked and shifted under the weight of difficult circumstances. Yet the second man—the Christian—had built his life and marriage on eternal values.

GOD'S IMPORTANCE IN MARRIAGE

Whenever I think back on that experience, I realize just how important it is for a couple to have God at the center of their marriage, to have Him for their foundation. With the scores of difficulties they can face—the extended illness of a spouse, the loss of a job, the anguish of losing a child—couples need to be able to see *all* of life from God's perspective. Every Christian couple, therefore, should diligently seek to grow together in God.

But having a positive attitude toward life's difficulties isn't the only reason couples should seek to develop a strong spiritual life. A number of other scriptural promises apply to couples whose marriage is given to the Lord. In the

Psalms, for instance, we find that, "Thy testimonies also are my delight; They are my counselors" (Ps. 119:24).

The church where I counsel is quite large. As a result, even though we have several counselors working there, people sometimes have to wait for up to two weeks to get an appointment. It is encouraging to know, then, that couples who study God's Word always can find a source of sound counsel—even without an appointment!

Elsewhere in Psalm 119, we read, "I understand more than the aged, because I have observed Thy precepts" (v. 100). When I was studying Hebrew in seminary, I learned that the word "understand" can be interpreted as "to make space between."

In buying their first house, considering when to begin a family, or when facing a difficult medical decision, couples need to be able to separate—or "make space between"—fact and fiction, emotion and intellect. They need a clear understanding of their options. Whatever the situation, the truths and insights of God's Word can provide couples with trustworthy perspectives to guide their decisions.

Finally, by placing God at the center of a marriage, a couple can become part of a timeless triangle. Let me explain this concept a bit.

Have you ever seen a couple focus all their attention on one child? This commonly occurs when a newborn comes home, and it often draws a couple closer together. However, if parents continue to focus exclusively on that child—day after day, week after week—problems can develop. By continuously concentrating on a third person—even though that person is their own baby—a couple can forget to interact with *each other.* As a result, an emotional gap may develop between husband and wife.

By contrast, when a couple spends time focusing on Jesus Christ, the results are beneficial. As the years go by, and each spouse draws closer to Christ, they also will find themselves drawing closer to one another. In effect, by learning to love God, couples can learn how better to love each other. A timeless triangle has been established!

Now that we're aware of the important role God and His Word can play in a marriage, couples should be able to run out and start growing together spiritually, right?

Not necessarily.

The fact is, the ability to grow together in this area is never a "given"—even for committed Christian couples. What makes "couple closeness" in this vital area so hard to attain? Several potential problems merit consideration.

COMPETING INTERESTS

The first factor that can prevent couples from growing together spiritually is the problem of balancing one's obligation to care for a spouse's needs, with one's spiritual responsibilities to the Lord. Paul sheds some light on the dynamics of this conflict:

> But I want you to be free from concern. One who is unmarried is concerned about the things of the Lord. . . . but one who is married is concerned about the things of the world, how he may please his wife, and his interests are divided (1 Cor. 7:32-34).

In seminary, I studied under Dr. Bruce Waltke. His lectures on the Old and New Testaments were outstanding. And his prayers! I think I would have paid to take his courses simply to hear him pray; his conversations with the Father were—and are—lessons in loving communication.

During one of his inspiring prayers before class, though, Dr. Waltke asked God to forgive him for not always knowing whom he loved more—his Lord or his wife. After closing his prayer, he explained to us that as a husband, he had a responsibility to meet his wife's various needs. But as a Christian, he had a responsibility to devote his life and talents to God's service.

Occasionally, these competing needs would come into direct conflict for him—like the time he promised his wife he'd attend an important social function with her, then realized it was on the same night he had promised to provide extra help for some struggling seminarians. What promise would he honor? Would spending time with his wife come first, or would his ministry to his students?

His predicament is not unique. When we enter into marriage, another human being's emotional, physical, and financial needs all require our attention. Paul realized, however, that meeting a husband or wife's needs can compete with spiritual concerns. Consequently, the desire to honor our spouse's tangible needs sometimes can cause us to neglect our time with the Lord.

Does this potential conflict of interest mean that marriage will prevent a couple from having a close walk with the Lord? Certainly not. Couples *can* balance their interests and develop a deep spiritual life—both as individuals and as part of a husband and wife team. They simply need to remind themselves that the urgent demands of daily life and marital devotion must not drive out time for spiritual closeness—with one another or with God.

If God has ordained marriage—and He has—He will give couples the wisdom and wherewithal to execute this delicate balancing act.

DIFFERING MATURITY
A second problem that can prevent couples from growing together spiritually is that of differing levels of spiritual maturity. A couple who recently came to me for counseling exemplified this dilemma.

Jim's family had a strong Christian background. He was the third generation in his family to be seminary-educated and he strongly wanted to enter the pastorate. With graduation only a few months away, though, he found himself wrestling with a genuine concern over his future ministry. This concern had to do with his wife's spiritual life.

Janet had begun her college career at a large secular university. During her sophomore year there, she came to know the Lord through the ministry of Campus Crusade for Christ. This was her first exposure to the Gospel; as a child, her family had never expressed any interest in spiritual matters.

As she evaluated her plans and goals for that year, Janet eventually decided to attend a Christian liberal arts college. It was there, as a very young believer, that she met Jim.

Initially, Jim's devotion to spiritual matters was a tremendous attraction to this young lady. She had never known anyone like him before and gladly took on the role of the "student" to his "teacher." Eventually, they married—their respective roles intact. Before long, however, this arrangement led to some problems.

Janet, for example, tried valiantly to study books on key doctrinal issues. She wanted desperately to come up to her husband's level of spiritual knowledge. Jim, meanwhile, felt that as the "teacher," he was responsible to provide his wife with a never-ending stream of theological information. So he began delivering tedious, hour-long lectures on *everything* he was learning at seminary. Night after excruciatingly dull night, he explained the intricacies of transubstantiation, the marvels of thirteenth-century scholasticism, the shortcomings of German high criticism.

Finally, after Janet fell asleep during one of these "quiet time lectures," Jim realized they needed to seek some outside counsel. He was genuinely concerned with Janet's spiritual life. Yet before marrying her, he had completely failed to consider their vast differences in biblical knowledge and experience. He hadn't foreseen the types of problems these differences would generate.

Admittedly, this couple represents something of an extreme. Yet many couples *do* set themselves up for failure in their effort to grow together spiritually by failing to make allowances for differing levels of maturity.

This is particularly true in situations where the *wife* is the spiritually "stronger" of the two. I have seen several cases where a husband has given up his biblical responsibility to be the spiritual leader in a marriage (Eph. 5:23) simply because he felt he couldn't measure up to his "learned" wife's expectations.

This is not to say, though, that one spouse should discontinue his or her own study of Scripture to allow a partner to "catch up." Rather, Paul encourages us to continue our walk with God, but to do so "with all humility and gentleness, with patience, showing forbearance to one another in love" (Eph. 4:2). By following this teaching, differences can be bridged and a deeper level of mutual spiritual maturity achieved.

LIVING ON YESTERDAYS

Exodus 15 has long been a favorite Old Testament chapter of mine. After miraculously passing through the Red Sea, Moses and the nation of Israel paused to sing, "Thou didst blow with Thy wind, and the sea covered them; They sank like lead in mighty waters. Who is like Thee among the gods, O Lord?" (Ex. 12:10-11)

But beginning with verse 22, we read that in the wilderness of Shur, the Israelites "found no water." Even when they did find it, the water was at Marah, called "bitter" in Hebrew, where it was undrinkable. Suddenly, this assembly of people—who had seen God part a sea to meet their needs only three days before—began grumbling to Moses about not having anything to drink. God had provided miracles in the past. Where was He now?

Before we become intolerant and upset at their outcry, we should recognize how easy it is for us to exhibit this same attitude in our married life. God's chosen people thought they could live off past spiritual triumphs and miracles. They didn't realize that to receive God's continued blessing, they needed to be obedient to Him on a daily basis.

Similarly, many couples have seen God's hand direct their steps toward marriage in a very obvious way. Others have recognized His tangible blessings at some point in their relationship. So in the "wilderness periods" of marital life, these couples expect to rely on yesterday's spiritual "highs" to carry them through today's spiritual "low."

Certainly, we need to thank God for what He has accomplished in our marriage in times past. But if we're facing *current* marital trials, we must learn to seek His provision for our marriage *today*. We cannot rely on "yesterdays"—however wonderful they were—to help us grow together spiritually in the here and now.

YOUR ADVERSARY, THE DEVIL

With all of these hindrances to spiritual unity, you might begin to suspect that someone's trying to prevent you and your spouse from growing together in Christ. Well, you're absolutely right: someone is! Behind each of these common obstacles, and a hundred others, stands a warning: "Be on the alert. Your adversary, the devil, prowls about like a roaring lion, seeking someone to devour" (1 Peter 5:8).

There's no question about it: Satan is a master of subtle manipulation. He doesn't need to attack married couples with a legion of shrieking demons to keep us from growing together spiritually. Often, all he has to do is simply place some sort of obstacle in our way to make it "inconvenient" for us to focus on the Lord as husband and wife. Finding that we're "too busy" to pray with our spouse, or that we "just don't feel like" studying the Word together, could well be products of Satan's skillful machinations.

Is there anyway through Satan's labyrinth of deception? Indeed there is! God's Word states, "I am confident of this very thing, that He who began a good work in you will perfect it until the day of Christ Jesus" (Phil. 1:6). In short, we can stand assured that a marriage grounded in Christ is resistant to Satan; for truly, "greater is He who is in you than he who is in the world" (1 John 4:4).

GROWING BY STEPS, NOT LEAPS

Do you remember the second individual mentioned in this chapter's opening illustration? This older saint did not suddenly wake up at age seventy with a rock-solid faith. His relationship with the Lord had developed over a number of years; it was the result of many small steps of faith along the way.

Most married couples *want* to grow spiritually. Yet they are frustrated when their infrequent devotional times together do not result in great "leaps" forward. At this point, it is important to remember that our individual levels of spiritual maturity came through daily and persistent steps in a walk of faith. There was no express elevator to spirituality when we were single and there's no special rocket marked "For Couples Only" now that we're married. Couples need to recognize that growing together spiritually is a *process*. And like most processes, it requires commitment...and time.

CREATIVE TIMES TOGETHER
Since this process *is* so important, to conclude this chapter, let's look at some practical suggestions to help you and your spouse make your first steps toward mutual spiritual growth successful ones.

First, set aside a special time for spiritual togetherness. Morning or evening, once a day or once a week, consistency is the key. And in spending time together before the Lord— whether in prayer or Bible study—try to create an atmosphere that is conducive to such times together. Take the phone off the hook. Make sure the children are asleep. When outside distractions are minimized, your devotional time together can be even more profitable.

Second, I recommend that couples begin with realistic and confidence-building goals. I once talked with a couple whose goal for their first year of marriage was to read through the entire Bible. But when I spoke with them after ten months of marriage, they admitted they would need to read at least twenty chapters a day, every day, for two months—just to get through the Old Testament! They were about ready to abandon the entire project. Obviously, this

25

couple should have set their sites on a more realistic target. They could, for example, have listened to one tape a week by their pastor or by an expositor such as Charles Swindoll and followed along in their Bibles.

When it comes to setting spiritual growth goals, many couples act like forty-yard-dash men who are trying to run a marathon. They take on challenges they can't possibly accomplish. But couples who begin with feasible goals are much more likely to see success as they begin growing together spiritually.

Third, for the couple who falls asleep trying to have a detailed grammatical study of 2 Chronicles, I'd suggest having a picnic and bringing along Bibles. Outside in God's creation, a short time together in His Word often can accomplish more than hours of "forced" study. When we studied Genesis, my wife Cindy and I went to the local zoo. First, we had a sack lunch and read about how God created all living things. Then we took a "real-life tour" among His miraculous works!

Fourth, keep a current prayer diary. Cindy has kept such a diary for several years. It's amazing to see how exciting prayer can become when you record God's answers to your requests. Such a record also is a tremendous encouragement to look back on after several months have passed. It provides a tangible way to see how God's hand has been working in a relationship.

Finally, close the day with conversation together to the Lord. As you lie in each other's arms, recount your thanks for one another and for the day the Lord has given you. Such intimate conversations with our Lord can help you carve out a deep love for the Saviour—and for each other.

In sum, couple devotions do not have to be couple "demotivations." Jim Rayburn, founder of the Young Life ministry, often remarked, "It's a sin to bore a kid with the Gospel." While this may not be true in a strict sense, his comment contains an important truth. Many couples get bogged down in minute study programs early in their married life, get discouraged, then give up on the excitement of integrating the Lord Jesus into their relationship. This simply doesn't have to happen.

For couples who are patient, sensitive, inventive, and expectant, the rewards of spiritual times together not only will touch their own relationship, but will reach those around them. Kenneth Gangle, a widely known Christian educator, has said, "The greatest evangelical tool the church has today is a distinctively Christian home."

Why not begin today to mark your marriage as distinctively His? Why not begin today to grow spiritually? It's the foundation for growing together in all the other areas of your marriage.

EXERCISES IN GROWING TOGETHER

(1) Apart from the ones listed in this chapter, can you think of any other reasons why couples should seek to grow together spiritually? Find passages from Scripture which illustrate your reasons.

_____

_____

_____

_____

_____

(2) What has been the greatest obstacle to spiritual growth in your marriage? Have you had more than one? Can you list any not covered in this chapter?

_____

_____

_____

_____

(3) With your spouse, review the following questions, list *specific* answers to each, then actively apply them to your marriage.

(a) When would be the best time for you to meet together for devotions, prayer, or Bible study?

(b) What realistic, confidence-building goals should you set for your joint spiritual life for the next six months? For the next year?

(c) What type of creative approaches to spiritual togetherness can you integrate into your marriage?

(d) Have you ever kept a current prayer diary? If not, why not try it—at least for a month? Then, evaluate its helpfulness to your marriage.

_____

_____

_____

_____

(4) Refer to the Marriage Enrichment Program in Chapter Eleven for further helpful exercises.

THREE

The Importance of "Leaving" Home

They had been married only two years. Now, Brent and Carol sat in my office, teetering on the brink of divorce. The fact that their marriage had deteriorated so quickly was tragic enough. But in my opinion, this couple had experienced an even greater tragedy: they had failed to recognize the underlying *cause* of their marital problems. Oh, they knew which single incident had touched off their troubles. Yes, they both remembered that dreadful night before their wedding. Still, they couldn't understand *why* the aftermath of that one evening had led to the virtual destruction of their marriage....

Brent and Carol's courtship had been a brief one. As a result, their parents were extremely upset when they announced their plans to marry. On the night of their rehearsal dinner, both families finally vented their pent-up frustrations over this situation. Tearing into their future in-laws with angry and insulting words, each side blamed the other for encouraging this marriage. During a time normally set aside for festivity, a feud began instead. That night the two families resolved to avoid all contact with each other.

For the young couple, the results of this decision were disastrous. Carol's mother told her she could visit home only if "that boy"—her husband—did not accompany her. Brent's family treated Carol with the same steely contempt.

Unable to bear the loss of her mother's approval, Carol began to spend an increasing amount of time at her parents' home. Unwilling to accept Carol's parents—or her desire to be with them—Brent began spending entire weekends with *his* parents.

Now, nearly two years later, this couple still could not understand why the fight at their rehearsal dinner had resulted in their ongoing problems with one another.

Actually, the fight hadn't caused their problems at all. Rather, it was Brent and Carol's behavior *following* the rehearsal dinner fiasco that led to their trouble. When the battlelines were drawn that night, it was up to this young couple to remain united—and neutral. Yet their actions revealed that they still had a greater sense of loyalty and attachment to their parents than to each other.

Their experience is a classic example of what happens when a couple fails to integrate the biblical concepts of "leaving one's father and mother," and "cleaving to one's spouse" into their marriage. In effect, Brent and Carol's inability to "leave" their parents—to emotionally separate themselves from their parents' homes and to forge their own, autonomous identity—cut short their ability to cleave to one another. As long as this couple continues along this destructive path, there'll be no winners—only losers. Another marital casualty will have been racked up.

WHY WE MUST "LEAVE" HOME

In God's blueprint for married life, we see that *"leaving"* one's home is a prerequisite to *cleaving* to one's spouse. As alluded to earlier:

> For this cause a man shall leave his father and his mother, and shall cleave to his wife; and they shall become one flesh. And the man and his wife were both naked and were not ashamed (Gen. 2:24-25).

In these verses, "leaving" home is clearly identified as the first rung in a ladder leading to intimacy. Once this initial step is achieved, cleaving, becoming one flesh, and standing totally transparent before one's spouse become possible. Each of these steps reflects a progressive sense of closeness and concern between husband and wife. All are vital to the process of growing together, to the process of deepening and enriching a marriage.

But an attempt to move a relationship to these higher levels of commitment without first "separating" one's self from home and parents will lead only to frustration—as Brent and Carol's situation demonstrated. If a couple genuinely desires to cleave together, they cannot afford to ignore the process of "leaving" home.

HOW TO "LEAVE"

Since "leaving" home is so important, we ought to examine *how* to do it. One important way is to establish a "peer relationship" with our parents.

After church one Sunday, a newly married couple rushed up to me, excitement written across their faces. "It was wonderful!" Gerry blurted out. "Last night, Molly and I double-dated with my parents. In twenty-four years, it was the first time my father and I ever related to one another as equals."

Gerry was lucky. He wanted his father to recognize that their relationship had undergone a change following his marriage to Molly. They still were father and son, of course; but Gerry now was a married man with his own responsibilities to handle. Fortunately, Gerry's father realized his son no longer was a boy and readily accepted him as a peer.

This concept of relating to one's parents as peers can be difficult—both for grown children and parents. Years of looking up to parents as authority figures certainly can make this process an awkward one. I felt this myself in my relationship with my father.

Can you imagine anyone being excited over the opportunity to pay a lunch bill? Well I was. For years, whenever we went out to eat, my dad never let me pick up the check. Every time I even *tried* to snatch up the bill, he would wrestle it away from me. Back then, the message, "I'm the father, I pay for my childrens' meals," was not to be challenged.

But after getting married, moving away, and taking on the responsibilities of being a husband, my father finally let me pick up the tab. He had come to see me as a peer. And, what with the high cost of eating out, perhaps he had seen some advantages to that!

What's important, though, is that I knew I had successfully "left" home when my efforts to establish a peer relationship with my parents paid off. Allowing me to pay for lunch was my father's unspoken way of acknowledging this new relationship.

Couples should try to find ways, then, to develop peer relationships with their parents. The double-dating idea mentioned earlier is a good one. So is having a Bible study with your parents and/or in-laws. Basically, any activity that allows a married couple to relate to their parents as *adults* is helpful.

To "leave" home, we also need to resolve long-standing tensions between ourselves and our parents. Unresolved tensions tie us to the past, they keep us emotionally chained to our parents' home, they spill over into our marriage. Yet resolving these problems allows us to put familial difficulties behind us, frees us to establish a healthy relationship with our parents, permits us to "leave" home, and lays the groundwork for couples to grow together.

I once counseled a husband whose inability to deal with bitterness toward his parents was wreaking havoc on his marriage. Every other word out of Tim's mouth concerned how terrible his home life had been. His bitterness over this situation now was affecting his marriage, as well; as his frustrations consumed him, he was becoming increasingly impatient and uncaring toward his wife.

To help Tim better understand his background—and to help him unravel the source of his bitterness—I told him to bring as many old family photographs as he could to our next counseling session. When he came in the next week, he had an entire shoebox full of vacation, holiday, and other typical "growing up" snapshots. What surprised me most about these pictures was that everyone in them looked *happy*. In contrast to what Tim had told me, these pictures seemed to indicate that he had been very loved and accepted.

About halfway through our session, Tim suddenly broke down and began to cry. In the presence of his wife and myself, Tim explained that *he* had been the one who turned his back on his family. *He* had rebelled as a teenager and severed all relationships with his family. Years of regret and guilt had made him deny and reverse the facts of his story. However, when he stopped long enough to remember—to remember the *truth*—he finally was able to put aside his anger and see things clearly. He could break his painful ties to the past and their hurtful effect on his marriage. He could, in fact, "leave" home.

You may never have experienced the type of profound resentment Tim felt toward his family. Yet you may be feeling *some* sort of unresolved anger or bitterness toward one, or both, of your parents. Incidents which occurred years ago may still infuriate you. If so, those particular experiences are preventing you from "leaving" home; those unresolved events still have at least part of you locked securely in your parents' home.

Therefore, I think it might be helpful to take a moment to review the basics of the "remembering" process Tim used to successfully "leave" home.

First, like Tim, take a long afternoon to go over some family photo albums with your spouse. Some people—particularly shy ones—can't stand to let others see them in "bearskin rug" poses. However, if you avoid going back through old home movies or snapshots, you'll be depriving yourself and your spouse of a much-needed view of the past.

Discuss why the situation depicted in the picture was photographed. Take note of who is always in the pictures, and who is left out. A visual depiction of a person's family tree can be a tremendous aid in illustrating family dynamics—and how they've affected that individual.

Also, be sure to make the most of your visits back home with relatives. Ask questions about how your parents met, what their family life was like, and what tensions *they* experienced in the past. Often, a parent or relative welcomes the opportunity to discuss important family events, and a couple can gain much from interacting with them.

The point of all these activities, of course, is to try to identify any areas of unresolved tension between you and your parents. If there are none, congratulations— you're among the lucky few! But if you *do* find some trouble spots, you should work to resolve them immediately. Talking to your parents about past problems in a nonaccusatory and constructive manner can be an important first step.

WHAT "LEAVING HOME" IS NOT
We've now examined why it's important to "leave" home, and discussed two practical ways to do so. I'm saddened to report, however, that many married persons try to "leave" home in incorrect and damaging ways. Apparently, there are quite a few counterfeit ideas circulating about what it means to "separate" ourselves from our parents; and some couples—Christians included—have embraced these notions.

I think it's necessary, therefore, to look at what "leaving" is *not*, in order to better understand what genuine, biblical "leaving" *does* mean.

First, "leaving" home does not mean cutting off all contact with one's home. A number of secular authors recommend severing relationships with one's parents as an aid to setting up an independent identity; couples must "leave the nest" once and for all if they're to be free. While this may make sense from a secular standpoint, it totally contradicts biblical teachings concerning parent/child relationships.

Jesus Himself spoke strongly against those who would follow such popular traditions rather than God's teaching:

> He was also saying to them, "You nicely set aside the commandment of God in order to keep your tradition. For Moses said, 'Honor your father and your mother'...but you say, 'If any man says to his father or his mother, anything of mine you might have been helped by is Corban (that is to say, given to God),' you no longer permit him to do anything for his father or his mother; thus invalidating the Word of God by your tradition which you have handed down" (Mark 7:9-11).

I have seen a number of couples follow the "Me" generation's tradition and refuse to have any contact with their parents. As a result, they've created an icy state between themselves and their folks that probably will last for years. I only can hope that someday, these couples will realize a simple fact: They must be able to relate to their parents in a responsible fashion *before* they successfully can "leave" home.

Second, "leaving" home does not mean we regard our parents' counsel as obsolete or outdated. Some couples believe they'll gain true independence only after they've learned life's lessons through their *own* experiences. Parents are invited to keep their opinions to themselves.

In our society, we hold the discomforting belief that if something's old, it's useless. If a product on the grocery shelf doesn't have a "new and improved" label on it, something must be wrong with it. My twin brother, a cancer researcher, recently told me he relies almost exclusively on *frequently* published professional journals for his research information. If the information he needed were put into book form, it would be outdated by the time the book was published. In other words, old information is useless information.

Many couples, unfortunately, believe that principles which are relevant to selling groceries and preparing research journals also apply to their relationship with their parents. These couples feel it's passé to accept the counsel of parents who remember the Great Depression as an event, not simply a test question. They imagine that if they scorn their parents' advice and learn everything from firsthand experience, they'll truly have stepped out on their own.

But in the Book of Proverbs, we see that older persons are valuable and their wisdom is praiseworthy:

> Listen to your father who begot you, and do not despise your mother when she is old (23:22).

And in Job we find:

> Wisdom is with aged men,
> With long life is understanding (12:12).

Most parents have gone through the proverbial "school of hard knocks" and have acquired their wisdom the old fashioned way: they've *earned* it! So when it comes time to make an important decision—such as purchasing a house or taking out a second mortgage—it's nice to be able to seek the opinion of someone who's traveled down life's road (and who is well-acquainted with its bumps!)

Third, "leaving" home does not mean we behave like two-year-olds. What do I mean by this? Well, when a child is at that tender age, and his or her mother says, "Don't touch the stove, it's hot," the child's course of action is simple. He or she listens to the command, pauses, then goes right ahead and touches the stove!

This is the same type of logic many adults employ in their efforts to "leave" home. "If I simply do the opposite of my parents' wishes," they reason, "that will prove I'm independent." Esau was someone who seemed to be quite a fan of this approach.

As the firstborn, Esau knew Isaac's instructions concerning the marriage of his sons. They were to take wives from those in the land of Isaac's father, wives who believed in God and were of the household of faith (Gen. 26:3). Esau's brother, Jacob, had obeyed this instruction and found Rachel. Esau, however, desired to set up his own home, in his own way.

> Then Esau married Judith the daughter of Beeri the Hittite, and Basemath the daughter of Elon the Hittite; and they brought grief to Isaac and Rebekah (Gen. 26:34).

By marrying foreigners, by doing exactly what his parents *didn't* want him to do, did Esau really demonstrate independence? Not in the least. The fact is, when he saw that his actions upset his parents, Esau married another, more acceptable wife in an effort to win back their approval (Gen. 28:8-9). Some independence!

Let Esau's mistake be a lesson to us. Simply contradicting our parent's wishes will not make us more mature or independent. Rather, when we stop "putting our hands on hot stoves," and work at establishing peer relationships with our parents, then we'll know the true meaning of "leaving" home.

As we close this chapter, we need to look at the last, and probably the most common, counterfeit definition of "leaving" home. This definition states that *distance* from one's family equals *detachment.*

In *On Golden Pond*—a film that deals with family relationships—the daughter makes a statement about her father: "He's still controlling my life. I live 2,000 miles away and he's still controlling my life." Sound familiar?

Putting miles between you and your parents does not necessarily indicate that you've "left" home. I've known couples who lived halfway around the world from their parents—and they *still* suffered from unresolved problems with them.

It should be clear by now that "leaving" home is a process. It takes time and effort, not just distance. It takes a commitment to establish peer relationships and to resolve tensions. Hopefully, lessons in "leaving" begin when a son or daughter is granted appropriate responsibilities and independence early in life. For some couples—such as Brent and Carol—this process never begins. And in light of the disastrous outcome of their failure to "leave" home, I must reemphasize the following points. Unless we "leave" home, cleaving cannot occur. Unless we cleave, growing together will be impossible.

However, before we examine what it means to cleave together as husband and wife, we first need to stop in several "hard-to-leave" homes. These are homes in which the methods for "leaving" described in this chapter may not be sufficient. These are homes in which special problems require special attention before a person successfully can "leave" home.

EXERCISES IN GROWING TOGETHER

(1) Discuss how you feel about the whole notion of relating to your parents as peers. If you feel uncomfortable about this idea, explain why. If you feel at home with it, explain that, as well. How do you think your answer to these questions will influence your ability to "leave" home?

_____

_____

_____

_____

(2) What specific steps could you take to establish—or improve—a "peer relationship" with your parents and/or in-laws? List several.

_____

_____

_____

_____

(3) Are there any areas of unresolved tension currently existing between you and your parents? If necessary, use the "remembering" technique described in this chapter to help you identify them.

  (a) Once you decide what tensions still exist, list them, and describe the particular emotions they produce in you.

  (b) Pick a *specific* time in the *near future* to discuss your findings and feelings with your parents. If your parents are deceased, talk to a pastor or counselor about this subject.

_____

_____

_____

_____

(4) This chapter looked at several poor ways to "leave" home.

  (a) Have you ever used any of these methods? Which ones? Why?

  (b) What insights can you gain about your relationship with your parents given your response to (a)?

_____

_____

_____

_____

(5)Refer to the Marriage Enrichment Program in Chapter Eleven for further helpful exercises.

FOUR

"Hard-to-Leave" Homes

Have you ever watched a young child imitate his or her parents? The results can be pretty amusing. My niece, for example, really loves her dad and wants to be just like him. That's why at age four, she decided to take up shaving. She enjoyed seeing her dad go through his early morning ritual as he prepared for work and she carefully watched him execute each step of the shaving process. It came as no surprise, then, when she announced that *she* wanted to start shaving too. Before long, she was joining her dad in front of the mirror—a little lather on her chin, a toy razor in her hand.

It has been said that imitation is the highest form of flattery. And in my little niece's case, that saying proved true. Yet imitation doesn't always produce such rosy scenes; in fact, imitation at times can lead to misery.

As we noted in the last chapter, painful experiences from our past can continue to haunt us in the present. They can keep us from "leaving" home and prevent us from growing together as husband and wife. And when we fail to resolve them, they're likely to be imitated and perpetuated in our marriage. A study on child abuse revealed, for instance, that over 80 percent of those arrested for this offense reported that *they* had been abused as children (D.J. Owens and M.A. Strauss, "The social structure of violence in childhood," *Aggressive Behavior,* vol. 12, 1975, p. 68). In effect, their failure to deal with a painful past had caused these persons to imitate their parents' behavior—with deadly results.

We also noted in chapter three that there are ways to resolve these long-standing problems. But is it *really* possible to break away from a past in which child abuse was a problem, or from which long-term psychological and emotional scars resulted? Can we *ever* really "leave" such homes?

While it may be a difficult process, it *is* possible to "move away" from homes in which particularly severe problems existed; there *is* hope for people who don't want to imitate their parents' mistakes. God's Word has a great deal to say to individuals who've come out of an especially painful past or a "hard-to-leave" home. For one, we're not simply to blame everything on our parents (Rom. 1:30). While venting anger against parents may bring short-term relief, it does little to resolve long-term problems. The Scriptures show us how to relate to our past and our parents in ways that will make a lasting difference. And once these problems are resolved and we're finally able to "leave" home, the joys of growing together can begin!

ROADBLOCKS
Before we look into the past and categorize different types of homes, we first need to recognize two roadblocks that may prevent us from doing so.

The first roadblock to dealing with our past involves the act of "remembering," itself. Researchers performed an interesting study several years ago, in which they sought to understand how the brain stores memories of past events. Through electrical stimulation, these researchers activated certain areas of the brain which they thought might "hold" memories. To the researchers' delight, many experimental subjects recalled memories with striking clarity, even if the events had occurred years earlier.

As the experiment progressed, however, an unexpected side effect developed. The subjects not only *recalled* a particular event, but experienced some of the *feelings* associated with that memory as well. For example, if the memory was of an emotionally painful experience, the subject actually reexperienced its pain (Wilder Penfield, *The Mystery of the Mind*, Princeton University Press, p. 148).

Many people avoid remembering difficult home situations precisely because it is painful to do so. Yet memories buried deep within us never can be brought before the Master Physician; they never can be brought out into God's healing light. We must be willing, therefore, to bring them out into the open and endure the pain of unpleasant memories if we're to resolve them once and for all.

A second barrier to opening up the past involves a protective instinct we feel toward our parents. Several years ago, I worked with an organization that shared Christ with high school students. That brought me, on a crisp November night, to a local stadium for the Friday night football game.

As I pulled into a parking space, a car full of teenagers roared up beside me and came screeching to a halt. Laughing and yelling, they piled out of the car and headed for the entrance gate. Unfortunately for the driver, I wasn't the only one who witnessed his rather wild driving; his father was parked in the space right next to mine. The father immediately leaped out of his car and began bawling out his son—right in front of the other kids.

When he finally finished his tirade and walked away, one of the guys in the car quipped, "Boy, your old man is messed up." That was all it took. Even though his father had just yelled at and embarrassed him, the young driver lashed out at this "outsider" who dared to speak against one of his parents. He told him—in no uncertain terms—to keep his mouth shut and to never speak that way about his dad again.

I have seen this same protective instinct exhibited time and time again. Regardless of the treatment we've received as children, when we become adults, a gut-level feeling that "these are the only parents I have" seems to take over. We become more willing to forgive all parental wrongs, to cover up all sins.

We all have a tremendous God-given love for our parents, and no one should parade a parent's faults around in public. But ignoring past problems with one's parents can prevent their cure. In fact, refusing to remember these problems is the best way to see them imitated in the present.

As difficult as it may be, married persons must resolve past difficulties if they are to "leave" home and cleave to their spouse. With this in mind, let's turn our attention to what life is like in four of the most common "hard-to-leave" homes.

DEPENDENCY BONDS

A couple experiencing conflict in their relationship can avoid dealing with their problems—and each other—in any number of "interesting" ways. One of the most popular is to focus all their attention on a child. By doing this, the couple is attempting to substitute an intense relationship with their child for an emotionally unfulfilling relationship with one another.

While this arrangement may at first seem beneficial to both parent and child, in reality, it usually causes the child to become enormously dependent on one, or both, of the parents. And once these "dependency bonds" are forged, they are not easily broken. As a result, "leaving" home becomes especially difficult.

A Christian child psychologist told me the story of Anna, a young girl who was the object of her mother's smothering attention.

True to the scenario presented above, Anna's parents' marriage was crumbling, and she had become the focus of all her mother's attention. Eventually, Anna began having a hard time relating to others at school. She seemed genuinely fearful of her classmates and even would run away from them when approached to play. An observant teacher noticed her behavior and recommended Anna see the school psychologist.

During their first meeting, the psychologist gave Anna a simple assignment. He told her to draw a picture of everyone in her family—but to leave herself out of the drawing. He carefully repeated the instructions and left Anna to draw the picture. When she turned in her drawing, the psychologist noticed that Anna had depicted every member of her family—except herself *and* her mother.

Again, the counselor instructed her to draw a picture of every family member *except herself*. Again, the picture came back with both Anna and her mother left out. Can you begin to see the pattern? Anna had become so emotionally bound to her mother that she couldn't leave herself out of the picture without leaving her mother out as well.

Unfortunately, children who have grown up under a parent's smothering affection can carry the results of this upbringing right into their marriage. One individual I recently counseled couldn't understand why his wife became so upset when he called his mother six or seven times *a day* to chat. Obviously, he was a victim of "dependency bonds." He simply could not loosen his attachment to his mother in order to draw closer to his wife. His adult behavior imitated his childhood experience. He could not "leave" home.

Children need to feel close to their parents—there's no denying that. Yet there is a marked difference between being a "special" child and being a "smothered" child. Persons who have grown up in this type of "hard-to-leave" home have a particularly difficult time transfering their attachments from a parent to a spouse.

LIFE IN—AND OUT OF—THE SPOTLIGHT
When one child repeatedly is singled out for special attention—in a family that includes more than one child—prob-

lems can result for *all* the siblings in this "hard-to-leave" home.

Perhaps the dynamics of this situation are best explained in the story of Joseph and his brothers.

> Now Israel loved Joseph more than all the other sons, because he was the son of his old age; and he made him a varicolored tunic. And his brothers saw that their father loved him more than all his brothers; so they hated him and could not speak to him on friendly terms (Gen. 37:3-4).

One of the beauties of Scripture is that it paints real life, warts and all. And here it shows how the preferential treatment Joseph received sparked irritation from his brothers; it shows how a father's desire to communicate love and acceptance to one son alienated a host of other sons.

In modern-day homes, the same story often is repeated. "Pretty," "athletic," or otherwise "special" children can entirely capture their parents' attention. This doesn't mean we should avoid shining the family spotlight on one child for some special reason. But if the spotlight *never* moves off that child, circumstances can conspire to create a "hard-to-leave" home.

And what exactly makes this home so difficult to "leave"? Consider the situation of the child living under the spotlight. Joseph lived with a privileged position at home; yet he never used his extra privilege to excuse a wrong or to take advantage of an unearned benefit. Others who find themselves under a spotlight, however, usually don't handle it as well.

Many adults who once were the center of attention in their families continue to carry selfish expectations into their marriage. After all, they were the star of their family. They were catered to. All their parents' attention revolved around meeting their needs. Now, they find a spouse telling them to get off the pedestal and start behaving responsibly. Suddenly, their old home starts looking a lot more attractive than their marriage. *I was treated great back* there, they think. *Maybe it wouldn't be so bad back* there. When this occurs, emotional and/or physical withdrawal from a spouse can take place.

This particular arrangement also can create a "hard-to-leave" home for the children who are left *out* of the spotlight.

Do you remember Joseph's brothers? Like most children, they were incredibly sensitive. While Israel, their father, loved them dearly, all they could see was that he loved Joseph more.

Today, children who always are left out of the spotlight can experience the same sense of insecurity and anger. In fact, an inability to *ever* feel completely accepted often results. This creates difficulties when a child grows up and marries; a spouse has to try to make up for years of parental neglect. And sometimes, no matter how hard a loving spouse tries, these individuals never believe they're truly accepted.

Every child needs to feel unique and special. But in a home where the spotlight never moves off one particular child, the unresolved bitterness and frustration that neglected children feel toward their parents can make this a difficult home to "leave."

ROLE REVERSALS
The fifth chapter of Ephesians is well known for its teachings on marriage and marital roles. But other biblical passages address these subjects, as well. Tucked away in the Song of Solomon, for example, is a tremendous description of what leadership in the home should be like.

As the couple in this book begins their marriage, Solomon's bride says, "Draw me after you and let us run together" (1:4). This wise woman was asking Solomon to be the leader of their relationship, and to draw her alongside as a partner, helper, and friend (S. Craig Glickman, *A Song For Lovers*, IVP, p. 31). They were to be companions, with

Solomon assuming the role of the loving leader, and his bride, the role of the valued partner.

But what happens in homes where this biblical model is ignored, where the wrong person "rules the roost"? Often, when leadership roles are reversed, patterns can be established that create a "hard-to-leave" home.

Take Susan and Mark's marriage. Susan came from a home where her mother had dominated nearly every aspect of her father's life. When it came to the children, finances, the social schedule, or vacations, her mother called the shots.

By the time Susan was in college, she already had decided what kind of man she would marry. He would not be passive like her father, but a strong leader she could follow. When she met Mark, Susan was convinced he fit the bill perfectly: he had been a college football player, he was the strong, silent type. Yes, there was no question about it: Mark was the man for her.

What Susan didn't realize, was that Mark came from a home which was very similar to her own. Since business occupied most of his father's time, Mark's mother had inherited all responsibility at home. Mark, as a result, did not have a strong biblical example of what a husband's role in marriage should be. He *did* exhibit leadership and drive whenever he played sports; but as soon as he walked into the house, he put everything into neutral. He didn't want to be a leader. He wanted to relax. Just like his father.

I'm sure you can picture the kinds of problems this young couple experienced. Susan found herself having to "take charge" at home—and began resenting it. Just like her mother. To avoid Susan's constant pleas that he be a leader at home, Mark began spending more time at work. Just like his father.

In only two short years, this couple was imitating the painful patterns of their parents' marriages—patterns their parents had taken *years* to perfect.

Exhausted and unfulfilled, this couple was at the point of

divorce. Fortunately, they finally stopped arguing long enough to see God's pattern for leadership in the home, and healing began to replace their hurts.

Like Susan and Mark, other couples face the same problem. Simply stated, they've come from homes where biblical leadership was not practiced; thus, they wind up imitating the only sort of marital roles they've ever seen—unhealthy ones. It's extremely difficult to put aside a lifetime of such exposure. It should come as no surprise, then, that it can be extremely difficult to "leave" this type of home—to put aside these old patterns and build a marriage based on the Bible's teachings.

UNSPEAKABLE HURTS, UNYIELDING CHAINS

It is estimated that as many as 1.5 million children in the United States have suffered some form of parental abuse. As noted at the beginning of this chapter, an incredibly high number of these children will, in turn, abuse their own children.

Yet when physical, sexual, or emotional abuse occurs at home, it all too often goes ignored. What desperately needs to be talked about becomes that terrible "family secret." All the while, the victims of abuse carry a stabbing pain in their heart and their anger toward their parents swells.

The memory of child abuse rarely fades. And the anger, bitterness, guilt, and frustration associated with this experience rarely disappears unaided. It endures through time; it spans the miles. Without saying too much more on this topic, then, I think it's easy to see why a home in which a person has been abused is the hardest home of all to "leave."

LEAVING A "HARD-TO-LEAVE" HOME

Each of the homes at which we've stopped, and many others, can prevent a married person from cleaving to his or her spouse. Because of the hurtful patterns established in each of these homes, many married persons find it hard to "move away" from them. Obviously, the few pages on "leaving" presented in this book will not spell an end to years of personal struggle. But they can mark the beginning.

By following biblical guidelines, couples can begin to cope and find God's hope. With this in mind, let's look at several principles that can help us deal with the past, break our ties to "hard-to-leave" homes, and prepare us for the excitement of growing together.

First, be aware that "leaving" takes place over time, not overnight. Proceeding patiently is the best advice I can give to those beginning the process of "leaving" home. If you rush up to your parents and pour out years of pent-up frustrations, you're certain to meet resistance—not acceptance. When you decide to "move away" from a difficult situation, you must understand that your parents have to make adjustments, as well. This fact explains why the next principle is so important.

Start praying daily for the healing of past relationships. The Holy Spirit still is in the business of changing hearts, and prayer still can make a difference in people's lives. It's always difficult for a parent or child to admit that their relationship is in need of repair, that parts of their past contain unhealthy elements. Some people will have to deal with the uncomfortable emotions of pride, anger, and guilt. But bathing your family in prayer will build up a foundation of love—a love that can help you cope with your past.

Third, supplement the missing sense of closeness you've felt toward your parents, with your Heavenly Father's love. I once worked with a woman whose parents divorced when she was in her early teens. She hadn't seen her father since. But every night, she read the last letter he wrote to her before the divorce. This one letter became her thin lifeline to a sense of family unity.

We need to be honest with ourselves when we deal with the past. Rereading old letters won't restore a fragmented family. It is infinitely more helpful to look to our Heavenly Father as a *present* source of help and encouragement. The more "at home" we are with our Lord, the more patience, acceptance, and endurance we can demonstrate to our earthly parents.

A fourth step toward "leaving" a difficult home situation involves our willingness to trust people again. This is particularly important for those who have come from a home in which they were abused. In homes where abuse was substituted for affection, it is difficult to learn the skills needed to form lasting, stable relationships. After all, if trust can be broken within the sanctuary of one's home, how can a person trust individuals in other relationships—including marriage? Can a person who has grown up in such a situation *really* learn to love again? After having been hurt, can he or she choose a response other than to hit back?

Jonathan proved that all these questions can be answered with an emphatic yes! Even though he came from a home in which he had been mistreated, Jonathan took the risks necessary to trust others.

His father, King Saul, was frustrated by personal failures and was terribly envious of David. So Saul reacted as many irritated parents do: he took out his anger on his child.

> Then Saul's anger burned against Jonathan and he said to him, "You son of a perverse, rebellious woman! . . . Therefore now, send and bring him [David] to me, for he must surely die." But Jonathan answered Saul his father and said to him, "Why should he be put to death? What has he done?" Then Saul hurled his spear at him to strike him down (1 Sam. 20:30-33).

Jonathan lived under his erring father for years. He easily could have hidden behind the hurt he suffered and never bothered to care for, or trust, another person again. Yet when he met David, Jonathan established a relationship that stands out as a classic portrait of brotherly loyalty and love.

Listen to the words of a man who could have had a heart

filled with hate, yet decided to break away from his hurtful home:

> And Jonathan said to David, "Go in safety, inasmuch as we have sworn to each other in the name of the Lord, saying, 'The Lord will be between me and you, and between my descendants and your descendants forever'" (20:42).

Did you notice the important element that formed the basis for their relationship? It's found in the words, "The Lord will be between me and you." Jonathan's Heavenly Father *already* had met his deepest needs. As a result, in spite of a painful home situation, Jonathan could "move away" from it; he could establish a relationship in which he loved David "as he loved his own life" (20:17). The lessons of this moving story, I believe, can be applied to any home situation. We too can learn to love our parents; we too can learn to trust others.

Once a person has dealt with the realities of his or her past, it's time to go to family members to put things right. Of course, this is easier said than done. We face a great challenge here: we're confronting our parents with potentially explosive feelings—yet we're trying to do so in an understanding manner.

However, this critical step *is* possible. We can use time spent on a family vacation, a special trip, or even a conference call on the telephone, to look at the past and to reexamine painful situations *as a family*. If necessary, a pastor or Christian family counselor can be called on to facilitate such interaction.

I've personally met with many families who were going through this delicate process. And I've seen steps taken toward resolving issues that had been left festering for years. I've actually seen people "leave" a "hard-to-leave" home! Friends, it *can* be done!

Don't just *assume* that your family would be unwilling to gather for this purpose. When old issues finally come out in the open, many family members actually are eager to discuss them. A commitment to love our family, and the patience to let God guide this important process, can help us say good-bye to a "hard-to-leave" home.

WINNING THE BATTLE

I'd like to close this chapter with a few words from a well-known hymn. Written by Martin Luther, the words of "A Mighty Fortress Is Our God" speak of a source of hope for persons engaged in the process of "leaving" a "hard-to-leave" home:

> Did we in our own strength confide,
> Our striving would be losing;
> Were not the right Man on our side,
> The Man of God's own choosing.
> Dost ask who that may be?
> Christ Jesus, it is He;
> Lord Sabaoth His name,
> From age to age the same,
> And He must win the battle.

EXERCISES IN GROWING TOGETHER

(1) Do you feel that you've come from any of the "hard-to-leave" homes depicted in this chapter? Since we often are not the most objective observers of our own background and behavior, you might ask your spouse whether he or she agrees with your conclusion.

_____

_____

_____

_____

(2) Obviously, not every type of "hard-to-leave" home could be discussed in one brief chapter. Therefore, apart from those mentioned here, are there any conditions in your past which are making it difficult for you to "leave" home? Again, ask your spouse to evaluate your response.

_____

_____

_____

_____

(3) In this chapter we examined several ways to "leave" a "hard-to-leave" home. Now, specifically apply these principles.

(a) In what ways will you need to be patient as you start the "leaving" process?

(b) What aspects of your relationship with your parents need the most prayer?

(c) What steps will you take to draw closer to God as you supplement a missing sense of family closeness with a closeness to Him?

(d) Describe areas in which you think trust has broken down between you and your parents. How can you constructively approach this problem and restore mutual trust?

(e) List several potential ways you could meet as a family unit to discuss family problems. Select the most feasible plan, and act on it!

_____

_____

_____

(4) Refer to the Marriage Enrichment Program in Chapter Eleven for further helpful information.

FIVE

Cleaving: A Concept for Courageous Couples

Every year, thousands of people travel to the tiny European nation of Monaco. Its spacious shops and lavish restaurants clearly account for a great deal of its popularity. But until recently, many tourists went to Monaco for at least one other reason: to try to catch a glimpse of Grace Kelly.

This young American actress had lived out the childhood fantasies of millions of women. After a three-day courtship, a real-life prince swept her away to live happily ever after. Talk about storybook endings!

Regrettably, many couples expect their marriage to exhibit this same fairy-tale quality. Vaulted expectations of what marriage will be like, egged on by Hollywood's projection of the perfect romance, serve as the model for today's marriages.

Yet in the midst of all this emotional pomp and circumstance, one fatal flaw often is ignored: in real life, marriage does not *end* with the prince winning his princess; it *begins* there.

The Prince and Princess of Monaco evidently realized this fact. From all accounts, they did not simply rely on fairy tales to preserve their marriage. Fashion designer Oleg Cassini, for example, has noted that this royal union lasted

"Because it was *not* a fairy tale. Fairy tales have a way of becoming undone."

How, then, do we explain the strength of their marriage? What kept this couple together until Grace's tragic death in 1982? Simply stated, I'm convinced that Princess Grace and Prince Rainer recognized the importance of one key concept: cleaving.

CLEAVING: A DEFINITION

I still can remember the first time I came across this word after becoming a Christian. It was in a verse mentioned earlier: "For this cause a man shall leave his father and his mother, and shall cleave to his wife; and they shall become one flesh" (Gen. 2:24).

I understood what "leaving" home meant. And I had a pretty good idea of what "becoming one flesh" entailed. But what in the world did "cleaving" mean? This Old English word was foreign to me. Perhaps it has puzzled you too.

To better understand this important concept, I think it would be helpful if we came up with a short definition of cleaving. As I see it, cleaving includes at least five characteristics:

- tenacious clinging
- sacrificial choices
- active commitment
- well-directed planning
- nurtured growth

Now don't panic! Some of these components may seem more confusing than the concept they represent. But if we examine one of them at a time, we should be able to get a fairly complete picture of what cleaving's all about.

TENACIOUS CLINGING

In God's Word, several verses shed some light on the concept of cleaving. The first is located in 2 Samuel 23:10. Here we find the story of Eleazer. While he's largely been forgotten in our day and age, during David's reign, Eleazer held a place of honor. As one of David's "mighty men," he, and only three others, had fought the Philistines in a crucial battle. Listen to the words that describe his actions:

> He arose and struck the Philistines until his hand was weary and *clung* (or *cleaved*) to the sword, and the Lord brought about a great victory that day (2 Sam. 23:10; italics and addition mine).

I recently had the opportunity to speak with a veteran of the Second World War. Of all his war-related remembrances, the one that stood out most in his mind involved his participation in the battle for the island of Guadalcanal.

Throughout the night, Japanese troops had been storming American positions. Hand-to-hand combat often ensued. As a result, the veteran told me, he needed constantly to be alert, to be on guard. When dawn arrived, and reinforcements came up from the coast, he finally had an opportunity to lay down his weapon. But he found he couldn't. He had grasped his rifle so intensely during the hours of combat that his hands had locked around the stock and barrel. A fellow marine had to help pry the gun from his grip.

Eleazer and this World War II veteran shared a common experience: both cleaved to their weapons to stay alive in the thick of the fight. Cleaving, therefore, denotes tenaciously clinging to something—or someone.

In marriage, cleaving to one's spouse should reflect this same sense of urgency. It too should be a matter of life and death.

Couples who are serious about cleaving face a number of determined foes: the daily lures of infidelity, the belief that monetary success justifies neglect of family, the notion that personal gratification comes above sacrifice. In essence, we live in a world full of loopholes just waiting to be applied to our marriage. And if each partner does not cling tenaciously to the other—like Eleazer to his sword, like the marine to his rifle—a marriage can be torn apart. We must never forget that apart from the Lord, our spouse is the most important person in our life. We are to guard that treasure diligently.

SACRIFICIAL CHOICES

A second use of the word "cleave" is found in the Book of Ruth. As this book begins, a terrible tragedy has taken place. Elimelech, an Israelite living in Moab, has died. In short order, his sons follow him to the grave. This left his wife, Naomi, and his two daughters-in-law without husbands.

According to the custom of the day, Naomi told her daughters-in-law to return to their own lands. Orpah, the wife of one of the sons, sized up her situation and decided to do just that. By returning home, she could receive her family's protection and perhaps marry again. Staying in Moab offered neither option.

Unlike Orpah, though, Ruth's commitment to her mother-in-law went far beyond personal convenience. Look closely at Ruth's actions.

> But Naomi said, "Return, my daughters. Why should you go with me? Have I sons in my womb, that they may be your husbands?" ... And they lifted up their voices and wept again; and Orpah kissed her mother-in-law, but Ruth *clung* (or *cleaved*) to her (Ruth 1:11, 14; italics and addition mine).

Ruth opted to stay with her mother-in-law. But in deciding to cleave to her, Ruth made a sacrificial choice: she sacrificed the security of her homeland to stay with Naomi. This obviously was not an easy decision for her to make.

Making sacrificial choices in marriage is just as difficult. Our society promotes "self," not sacrifice. Recently, a couple I know filed for legal separation. The husband's company had transferred him, but the move just didn't fit in with his wife's career plans. Since neither one was willing to sacrifice for the other, they simply decided to pursue separate paths. So much for the pledge of everlasting commitment they had made to each other at the altar only a year before.

Contrast their behavior to Jack and Beth's. He gave up a lucrative job with an ad agency so she could accept a fellowship at an out-of-state university. Jack knew how much Beth wanted to finish her Ph.D. So he made a sacrificial choice for her.

A second characteristic of cleaving, then, involves our willingness to make sacrifices when our spouse's best interest is at stake.

ACTIVE COMMITMENT

I came across an interesting definition of courage in my reading the other day. One anonymous author has called courage, "Movement in the face of fear." What often differentiates a hero from a person who hides is the simple fact that a hero is the one who gets up and moves—out of the foxhole to lead an attack, into the burning building to save a child.

Courageous couples are husbands and wives who also get up and move—to develop their relationship and grow together! In a world that urges us into the armchair of apathy, couples need to commit themselves to being actively involved in each other's lives.

This can be difficult to do—especially for couples with strongly developed and nonoverlapping areas of interest. Mike, for example, held a tenured position as a professor of political science at a large university. His wife Pam was a medical administrator at a prominent hospital. Both were so committed to their careers that problems soon developed in their marriage.

First, their hectic schedules kept them from spending a great deal of time with each other. And during the times they *were* together, they found that their increasingly specialized areas of interest left them with little to talk about. The thin layer of mutual interests they once had shared—camping, music, and reading—simply dissolved under the strain of their professional obligations.

Mike and Pam talked a great deal about commitment. The problem was, they were committed to their jobs, not to one another.

Scripture confirms the importance of active commitment within the context of marriage. God's Word clearly teaches that commitment is far different from mere verbal acknowledgment:

> The one who says, "I have come to know Him," and does not
> keep His commandments, is a liar, and the truth is not in him
> (1 John 2:4).

These are strong words when applied to our commitment to Christ. They're equally strong when applied to our commitment to our life's partner. An active commitment is one that tangibly demonstrates the reality of a person's words.

I recently had the privilege of leading a workshop at a Pro Athlete's Conference. A number of past and present sports celebrities and their wives attended; all had deep commitments to Christ.

During the workshop, one couple immediately caught my attention. Bill was an offensive lineman for an NFL team. He was so big that I fully expected him to block out the sun when he stood up. His wife Betty, at 5'4", seemed almost tiny by comparison. On the basis of physical appearance, I couldn't picture a more oddly matched pair. But in terms of their shared interests, this couple was but a heartbeat apart.

At lunch after the seminar, I sat at the same table with them. Out of curiosity, I asked Betty how much she knew about the position her husband played on his team. I expected her to say something like, "Oh, he's paid to stand in front of other people." Instead, I received a ten minute lecture on offensive blocking techniques. She concluded with a discussion on the finer points of pass protection blocking.

Somewhat dazed by her grasp of the sport, I had to ask

her how she had acquired so much knowledge. Betty explained that when she and Bill first were married, she grew to resent the time he spent at the practice field. Her favorite pasttime, in fact, was meeting with the wives of other players to complain about how neglected she felt.

As a Christian, this kind of negative attitude soon began to convict her. Eventually, Betty became convinced that she ought to take more of an interest in her husband's career, to become actively committed to what he did. So she began to ask Bill to explain aspects of football she didn't fully understand. She even spent several afternoons talking with assistant coaches, gaining more information about the intricacies of the game.

As she learned more about her husband's profession, Betty found herself becoming more of an encourager and support for him. As her perception of Bill's life came into clearer focus, she realized those long afternoons he spent practicing were no picnic. In all, Betty came away from the experience with a deeper commitment to her husband and their marriage.

With lunch almost over, I realized I hadn't had much of a chance to talk to Bill about this whole subject. But in our brief conversation, this enormous lineman made one comment I think I'll never forget: "Sometime I'll have to tell you how much Betty's taught me about refinishing antiques."

In this marriage, both husband and wife had mastered an important aspect of cleaving. Each was actively committed to his or her spouse's interests. The depth of love they shared clearly showed the benefits of this commitment.

Couples who wish to protect their marriage, as well as enrich it, need to develop shared interests. Pick out an area that interests your spouse and adopt it as one of your own. This is not to say, of course, that you shouldn't have *individual* interests. Just be sure there are some interests you can share as a couple. The ability to actively commit yourself to your husband's or wife's interests can lead both of you to a closer relationship.

WELL-DIRECTED PLANNING

Do you remember playing pin-the-tail-on-the-donkey as a child? Did you ever feel certain you were right on target—but when you took off your blindfold, the tail was in a less-than-appropriate place?

While it's fun to wander around in the dark during a party game, misdirected activity in a marriage is no laughing matter. Dan and Julie found this out through personal experience.

For some time, their marriage had been on an emotional roller coaster. Some days were great; others were terrible. Frankly, Dan and Julie were getting tired of this situation. They wanted to get off this frustrating ride. So after hearing a particularly challenging sermon on the family, they decided that "commitment" would characterize their marriage. They would start cleaving to one another!

Three months after they made their decision to cleave, they sat in my office, exhausted with the effort. What went wrong? Both Dan and Julie felt they had "given it their all." But as their story unfolded, we realized it was not their lack of energy that had sabotaged their attempt at growing. It was their lack of a well-directed *plan* for cleaving.

Basically, without discussing it with his wife, Dan decided that taking a special vacation with Julie would help them cleave together. Of course, this meant he had to take a part-time job to earn the money needed for the trip. But for Dan, the hours spent away from home were worth it. They would eventually yield a time of refreshment and romance. In Dan's mind, he was putting "deposits" into Julie's "personal account."

Without consulting Dan about *her* plans, Julie decided she could improve her cleaving skills by developing her spiritual life. Now that Dan was gone several evenings each week, she began spending time at a woman's Bible study. When Dan finally did come home, though, Julie was too busy preparing for her next Bible study to pay much attention to him. But in ways that made sense to her, each Bible study she attended was making a "deposit" into Dan's "personal account."

Earning extra money for a special trip and spending time studying Scripture certainly are not bad activities. However, neither Dan nor Julie had stopped to consider that their frenzied activities might actually be *hindering* their attempts at cleaving. Time spent away from a spouse hardly can be expected to facilitate the cleaving process.

But more importantly, they failed to realize that a couple cannot cleave unless they have a *joint* game plan for doing so. To cleave, both partners need to agree on how it will be done. For Dan and Julie, three months of *individual* activity left their relationship weaker, not stronger.

As I listened to their well-meaning but misdirected intentions, the Apostle Paul's words kept coming to mind:

> Do you not know that those who run in a race all run, but only one receives the prize? Run in such a way that you may win.... Therefore I run in such a way, as not without aim; I box in such a way, as not beating the air (1 Cor. 9:24, 26).

Dan and Julie certainly had been fighting hard to preserve their commitment to one another. Yet because neither sat down with the other and mapped out a well-directed plan for enriching their relationship, when they tried to draw on "accounts" into which they thought they had been making "deposits," they discovered a zero balance.

How can a couple avoid this situation? First, learn a lesson from Dan and Julie. Simply "doing things"—for, or with, one another—will not necessarily lead to marital cleaving. Taking time to fully understand the meaning of cleaving will. Second, don't just assume that you "know" what will fulfill your spouse's needs. Believe me, I learned this lesson the hard way.

Without consulting my wife, I made reservations for the two of us at a very expensive restaurant. Naturally, this meant I had to raid the money we had been saving to get a new sofa—but no problem! What Cindy really needed was a night on the town!

And so off to dinner we went. But as I looked at the brave little smile Cindy was wearing throughout the meal, I got the feeling something just wasn't right. Later in the evening, she gently told me she wished I hadn't spent so much money on a dinner when we had a greater need for a new sofa. Actually, she said, she wished we *both* had discussed ways to enrich our relationship. That really would have pleased her the most.

I learned a valuable lesson that night. Spending two months' savings on one night's dinner did not draw my wife any closer to me. I since have learned that taking time to understand *her* needs, and how she would like them met, is the best way to establish a well-directed plan for our relationship.

Proceeding without a well-established plan may make a parlor game more interesting or exciting, but it can wreak havoc on a marriage. As businessmen are so fond of saying, if we fail to plan, we might as well plan to fail.

NURTURED GROWTH

The final aspect of cleaving involves nurturing our spouse's growth. We need to help our husband or wife achieve success in each area of life—including the physical, emotional, intellectual, and spiritual. This idea is not the invention of contemporary psychology; it issues from the timeless Word of God.

As I mentioned earlier, the fifth chapter of Ephesians is one of the most familiar passages in the Bible. Yet often, we study only *half* of this key passage on marriage. Many people focus solely on verses 21-25, which deal with marital roles. The Apostle Paul, however, is concerned about the *quality* of the relationships that develop under these guidelines.

Specifically, Paul shows how one spouse's growth is inextricably linked to the other's:

So husbands ought also to love their wives as their own bodies. He who loves his own wife loves himself; for no one ever hated his own flesh, but nourishes and cherishes it, just as Christ also does the church, because we are members of His body (Eph. 5:28-30).

Clearly, Scripture gives our spouse's growth as high a priority as our own. Husbands and wives who see their spouse languishing from neglect might as well be ruining themselves. Yet as I counsel couples, I often notice the phenomenon of "one-sided growth": one person in a relationship is growing at the expense of the other. A husband is having a great time increasing his own knowledge at a Bible study; but somebody has to watch the kids—so the wife gets left home. When this occurs, a barrier—rather than a bridge—to cleaving is set up.

Please understand. This is not to say that the marital ledger must always be kept in perfect balance. There are times when one person *can* legitimately make special requests of his or her spouse. When one partner still is in school, he or she needs a spouse's financial support. When one partner is just beginning a new job, he or she needs extra understanding. During and after a pregnancy, a wife needs her husband's closeness and attention.

But growth opportunities should never consistently be limited to just one marriage partner. In God's program for growing together, both husbands and wives have a responsibility to nurture their partner's growth.

Ask yourself the following questions. What one thing could I do, beginning today, to help develop my spouse's intellectual life? emotional well-being? physical and spiritual health?

I know of one husband who has arranged to go to work late on Tuesday and Thursday mornings. This allows his wife time to meet several friends at an aerobics class; he stays home and keeps an eye on the kids. One woman in our church just started attending a local junior college. She's sixty. Her husband's loving encouragment allowed her to fulfill a lifelong dream.

Take time to ask your spouse about his or her dreams and goals. Then help him or her develop them.

Now that we've examined five aspects of cleaving, let's try to assess how well we've been practicing these essentials in our own marriage.

MEASURING MARITAL CLEAVING

Please take a moment to respond to the following questions. Circle the number that best represents the degree of cleaving currently evident in your marriage.

I cling tenaciously to my spouse (I try to keep outside distractions from separating us.)

1	2	3	4	5
Holding on by a few strands				Clinging tenaciously

I'm willing to make sacrificial choices for my spouse (I seek to put his or her interests before my own).

1	2	3	4	5
Put my interests first				Put spouse's interests first

I'm actively committed to my spouse in actions, not just words (I seek to understand his or her interests and encourage them).

1	2	3	4	5
Barely commmitted				Deeply committed

I've developed a well-directed plan for growing with my spouse (I include his or her input in these plans).

1	2	3	4	5
Make it up as we go				Clearly defined plan

I seek to understand my spouse's needs and am committed to nurturing them (I concentrate on emotional, intellectual, physical, and spiritual growth).

1	2	3	4	5
Little understanding			Deep understanding and commitment	

Now, for *really* courageous couples, ask your spouse to evaluate how well *he* or *she* thinks you're doing. Facing these five checkpoints of marital cleaving can be a real eye-opener and challenge. Several months from now, take this quiz again—particularly if you adopt the enrichment program in chapter eleven. It can be a good way to evaluate how well your love and commitment is developing for your spouse.

BURSTING THE BUBBLE
Marital commitment. Cleaving to our spouse. It doesn't come without effort, but the rewards are so great. It would be tremendous if every couple was deeply committed to the cleaving process. But truthfully, many couples reading this chapter are convinced they'll never be able to cleave to their spouse. They've realized their mate is just an ordinary person—not a prince or princess. As a result, they've allowed their feelings of love for their partner to fade. They're willing to give up.

Don't!

Listen to the words of a man who deals daily with this sort of problem. He recognizes the fallacy of depending solely on our feelings to guide us through marriage.

The myth of romantic love is a dreadful lie. When Mr. and Mrs. R acknowledge to each other that they have fallen out of love and then proceed to make each other miserable as they seek to regain their idea of "true love," they do not realize that their very acknowledgment could mark the beginning of the work of their marriage, instead of its end

(M. Scott Peck, *The Road Less Traveled*, Simon & Schuster, p. 92).

Why not burst the bubble of romantic deception? Why not reject the idea that a perfect, Hollywood-type relationship can be achieved with little or no effort? Why not turn away from the philosophy that says if you don't *feel* love for your spouse, cleaving to him or her will be impossible.

Substitute these ideas with a commitment to Christ and to your spouse. While dreams do offer a degree of satisfaction, a continuous, realistic commitment to cleave to your mate can be infinitely more vivid and fulfilling.

Isn't it time you woke up from a fairy-tale dream and asked God for the courage to cleave?

EXERCISES IN GROWING TOGETHER

(1) Discuss how you and your spouse can create a well-directed plan for increasing your sense of marital oneness. Decide what type of actions and attitudes will be necessary to facilitate cleaving. (Should you spend more time together every evening? Should you make a concerted effort to be less sarcastic with your spouse? Should you listen more attentively to your mate?)

_____

_____

_____

(2) Ask your spouse what one goal he or she most wants to accomplish during the coming year. Then, list ways you can:

    (a) become actively committed to your mate's goal; and

    (b) make sacrificial choices that will help your mate

achieve his or her goal.

_____

_____

_____

_____

(3) Individually, then with your spouse, mark your responses to the "Commitment Checklist" found in this chapter. On the basis of the responses you and your spouse made on the "Commitment Checklist," what aspects of commitment do you need to work on?

_____

_____

_____

(4) Refer to the Marriage Enrichment Program in Chapter Eleven for further helpful information.

SIX

Communication: Lifeblood of a Marriage

I've always been fascinated with the way the human body functions—and with how much it can teach us about relationships. Consider the circulatory system.

Each day, our heart pumps over 1,800 gallons of blood through 62,000 miles of blood vessels. This constant flow of blood distributes life-giving nutrients throughout the body. As long as this flow remains unobstructed, the body will stay healthy and continue to grow. Yet even a minor constriction of the circulatory system can create major health problems. If we ignore these problems and allow them to continue, our very life can be threatened.

Communication between a husband and wife is a great deal like the circulatory system. In a healthy marriage, communication flows unobstructed. Whether we're merely chatting, or sharing the deepest of dreams, our spouse understands what we're saying. But just as a junk food diet can clog our circulatory system, faulty communication patterns can impair a marriage.

Obviously, a single chapter on communication cannot hope to summarize the volumes of material written on this subject. But we *can* hit some of the high points. We can see what nurtures open dialogue and point out communication's most deadly enemies.

Before we begin, though, please let me make one observation. Open, effective communication is developed by practice. It is not something we receive as a wedding present, all wrapped up with a neat little bow. Reading about communication is one thing; actually experiencing it, doing it, practicing it—that's another.

The idea of having to *work* at communication may seem rather unusual to you. As I said before, it's something we more or less take for granted. But developing our communication skills is one of the most important things we can do if we are to grow together as a couple.

As we begin our look at marital communication, then, let's review three basic facts about this critical process.

WE'RE ALWAYS COMMUNICATING

Jimmy just couldn't understand what had gone wrong with his marriage. He was a good provider, a faithful spouse. He even managed to fit in time with his children. So why was his wife Becky so upset?

When this couple came to me for counseling, we sat down and tried to discover some of the factors that might be affecting their ability to communicate. In so doing, we uncovered a key decision Jimmy had made several years earlier.

Jimmy had come from a home filled with strife. His parents argued incessantly. Before he got married, he vowed that things would be different in his marriage. Jimmy decided that if he couldn't say anything positive to his spouse, he wouldn't say anything at all.

While this might seem like a good motto to live by, it actually worked to *hurt* his marriage. When a problem surfaced and it looked as though an argument was about to break out, Jimmy immediately would stop talking. Plain and simple. He'd just clam up. However, a 6'3" frame continued to talk for him. He'd let out a heavy sigh, cross his arms, furrow his brow, and stare off into the distance. That's all it took to drive Becky up the wall. *If we're having problems,* she'd think, *why won't this guy talk to me about them?*

What was their problem? Basically, Jimmy was unaware of the fact that people *always* are communicating—even when they're *not* talking. He mistakenly had assumed that his silence would halt communication. Actually, all it did was leave plenty of room for Becky to speculate—often incorrectly—about what was going on inside her husband's head.

Experts tell us that the bulk of what we communicate is "nonverbal." I believe it. In counseling sessions, I've actually seen a raised eyebrow make a spouse cry. Such small acts can be used to express unspoken feelings or frustrations.

The principle we need to learn from these examples is basic: deciding *not* to speak still can communicate volumes to another person. Our Lord, Himself, demonstrated the truth of this fact.

Unjustly arrested and falsely charged, Jesus stood before His accusers in silence. His failure to speak infuriated Pilate.

"Do You make no answer? See how many charges they bring against You!" But Jesus made no further answer; so that Pilate was astonished (Mark 15:4-5).

Jesus said nothing verbally. Still, He had effectively communicated His innocence to Pilate. In his heart, the Roman governor *knew* that he had been spoken to.

In marriage, couples can't take the Fifth Amendment and refuse to communicate. We're all constantly communicating. With that in mind, let's now look at a second basic element of communication.

BEWARE OF MIXED MESSAGES
My wife and I once saw a television commercial that left us in stitches. It pictured the winner of a beauty contest. This

lovely lady was smiling radiantly, joyously clutching a beautiful bouquet of flowers. As the camera moved in for a closeup, she gracefully turned to us and, without the slightest change in facial expression said, "My girdle is killing me!"

What made this particular commercial so effective was the disparity between her words and her actions. They just didn't go together. We weren't ready to receive a message that said, "I'm uncomfortable," when so much of what we saw communicated the opposite.

This "mixed message" made the commercial hilarious. In a marriage, such messages are anything *but* funny. When we transmit "mixed messages"—when our words and our actions communicate two different things—we're sure to give misleading and confusing impressions to our spouse. Let me use an example from my own experience.

I'm an avid (my wife often says *rabid*) football fan. When my favorite teams are on television, I must admit that I can get a little over-involved in the game. Consequently, if Cindy asks me to perform a minor chore or to help her with something during the game (the nerve of some spouses!), I have a typical response. I'll struggle through the words, "Sure Honey, I'm coming." But if you were to look at my facial expressions, you'd think I had just been operated on without an anesthetic. While my *words* say, "I'm available," my *nonverbal* behavior communicates exactly the opposite. It's saying, "If I have to get up from this game, we'll *both* be miserable."

Now, if I really were serious about facilitating honest, open communication, my course of action would be simple. I'd match my words with my unspoken message. In this case, I'd ask Cindy if the project could wait until after the game. If it couldn't, I suppose I *could* tear myself away from a few minutes of football.

Earlier, we saw that both words and nonverbal messages carry communication. The point here is, both verbal and nonverbal communication need to be consistent. Both need to be sending the same message.

This is no idle observation. It's extremely important to avoid "mixed messages." Research has shown, for example, that childhood schizophrenia occurs most often in homes where "mixed messages" are communicated. If children suffer emotionally in such homes, so will married persons. Repeatedly telling a spouse, "Nothing is wrong, I'm fine"— as you mope around the house—can lead to hurt and confusion.

Communication cannot grow when we say one thing, but do another. To keep communication lines unclogged, we need to reconcile our words with our actions. Both need to be clear.

SECURITY BREEDS SUCCESS

Most of us are hesitant to open our hearts to other persons. We wonder what they'll think after they've seen the "real me." Sometimes, we even find it difficult to express our true feelings to the Lord. Yet King David was a man who enjoyed open communication with his God. Listen to the honesty and candor he used in relating his feelings to his Heavenly Father:

> Be gracious to me, O Lord, for I am in distress; My eye is wasted away from grief, my soul and my body also. . . . I am forgotten as a dead man, out of mind. I am like a broken vessel. . . . Terror is on every side (Ps. 31:9, 12-13).

Elsewhere in this same Psalm, David explains *why* he is able to share his feelings in such an intimate manner:

> But as for me, I trust in Thee, O Lord, I say "Thou art my God." My times are in Thy hand (14-15).

David could open up his most heartfelt needs and frustrations to God because of the *security* he felt in their relationship. In the safety of his commitment to a compassionate, loving God, David was free to share both joys and burdens.

A third principle of communication, then, involves the ability to make our partner feel he or she can communicate without fear of rejection. We must establish a sense of security in our home before effective communication can occur. Let me ask you several questions. Is your home a place where feelings can be safely shared? Does there seem to be a lack of deep communication in your marriage? Are you making it easier—or more difficult—for your spouse to open up and talk with you?

Kevin and Dawn stumbled over these points in their relationship. Kevin was a chemical engineer and a very objective thinker. Whenever Dawn tried to share a sensitive feeling or concern with him, Kevin's engineering training jumped into gear. He would subject her emotions to analytical scrutiny. Were her feelings logical? Did they adhere to rational criteria? Could one "really" feel the way she did?

If Dawn persisted in trying to share her feelings, Kevin would give her a look that said, "End of conversation." It almost ended their marriage, as well.

Dawn *knew* how to think clearly. That wasn't her problem. What she needed was an understanding husband who could make her feel secure, who could listen to her, who could help her share her feelings.

We need to provide our spouse with the protection he or she needs to share deep feelings and needs. Our mate needs to know he or she can share emotions without fear of rejection or ridicule.

Let me encourage you to envelop your spouse with security. The more accepted and loved your life's partner feels, the more willing he or she will be to establish deeper levels of communication.

SEVEN GREAT WAYS TO KILL COMMUNICATION
So far, we've looked at three principles that are essential to effective communication. First, we must be aware that we are communicating with our spouse at all times, not just

when we're talking. Second, our verbal and nonverbal communication must be matched, not mixed. Third, open communication can develop only when our trust level is high enough to overcome our natural hesitancy to make ourselves known. These basic principles ought to be evident in our everyday marital communication.

Now, let's try to expand our understanding of communication a bit more. I'd like to do so, though, in a rather unusual way. I'd like us to look at seven things that can *prevent* effective marital communication from occurring. By learning how *not* to communicate, perhaps we can gain a few *positive* insights into this important process.

(1) *Make sure that when you're talking with your spouse, you're really communicating with someone else.* For years, Phil watched his mother recklessly spend every dime that came her way. When she died, her family was saddled with an enormous debt. Now, whenever Phil's wife Diane goes over budget—even if only by a few dollars—Phil reacts angrily. Yet Phil isn't really reacting to a present problem; he's responding to the past. He is, in effect, yelling at his *mother* for *her* fiscal irresponsibility.

Present problems also can affect our communication. Your boss yells at you for failing to finish a specific job. You come home and your spouse mentions that you've neglected to perform a promised chore. You respond by screaming at your mate to leave you alone. What does this reveal? Quite simply, you're verbally abusing your spouse in the way you wish you could abuse your boss.

The point of these examples is that our spouse occasionally may say or do something that reminds us of a person with whom we're angry. As a result, we speak to our mate as though he or she *were* that other person.

It's a fact: unresolved problems with other people *can* creep into our marital conversations. Yet each of us has only so much emotional energy; if we spend all our time angrily communicating with our spouse, we're in trouble.

If communication with your spouse tends to mirror this

pattern, I'd suggest doing at least two things. First, recognize that it's unhealthy to talk to your spouse as though he or she was the person who has angered you. Such behavior stifles effective communication and damages relationships. If you catch yourself doing this, bite your lip. Remember who it is you're *really* speaking with.

Second, talk to the individual with whom you're upset. Try to set that relationship right. If you can't talk with your spouse in a healthy manner because of problems you're having with someone else, you owe it to yourself and your spouse to get to the root of the problem.

(2) *Maintain an exaggerated distance between you and your spouse when you disagree.* Studies on marital communication show that communication between spouses drops as the distance between them increases. Think about a recent argument you've had with your spouse. The *physical* distance you maintained between one another probably was a good indication of the *emotional* distance you felt toward each other. And it's certainly difficult to communicate meaningfully with someone you're mad at.

When couples disagree, I encourage them to move closer together. I even suggest they hold hands when they talk. Why? Well, if you're close enough to hold hands, the need for shouting drops considerably. So does the need to flail your arms around to make a point. Emotions also become much less confusing.

In a scene from the movie, *Patton*, the general is angry because his troop advance has slowed down. With fury in his voice and dramatic gestures, he screams at his subordinates. His troops *will* continue to advance. If not, they will all die trying.

An aide approaches Patton and says, "General, you shouldn't talk that way. The men don't know when you're kidding."

"That doesn't matter," Patton replies. "It only matters if *I* know."

Angry words and gestures can result in similar confusion

in marriage. It's hard to see through a spouse's emotional displays to the real, underlying problem. Therefore, to turn this second communication killer around, why don't you try including a gentle touch in all your important talks—even if you're disagreeing. It can help calm the two of you down— and that always makes communication more enjoyable!

(3) *Use mental shorthand when you listen to your spouse.* Your spouse is struggling to express an important idea. You already know what he or she is trying to say, so *you* finish the idea. Wasn't that nice of you? You saved everyone *so* much time.

In almost every marriage, one partner is "quicker to the draw" when it comes to framing verbal messages. A real act of love, though, is to listen attentively to your spouse and patiently wait for him or her to finish speaking. The Book of Proverbs puts it in strong terms: "He who gives an answer before he hears, it is folly and shame to him" (18:13).

None of us has a crystal ball when it comes to communication. Even though we may be certain our spouse is expressing a thought we've heard 8,000 times before, we need to give our mate the gift of uninterrupted conversation. Even if the same old thing *is* being said, there may be a reason for it. Perhaps your spouse never felt you listened to or understood the issue the *first* time it came up.

You can correct this communication killer through simple patience. You won't regret the time you spend listening. It will pay rich relationship rewards to both of you.

(4) *Be ambiguous; never stick to any one topic; ramble as much as possible.* Some husbands and wives come from homes where vague, long-winded conversations were commonplace. Family members would ramble on and on about any number of things; and, if at the end of a discourse, they couldn't remember exactly what it was they'd been talking about in the first place, that was just fine. Unfortunately, many people who've come out of this type of environment now think that ambiguity is an acceptable way to communicate.

For communication to flow smoothly, though, it must take a *direct* path—regardless of the effort involved. One clear, straightforward, and concise statement can save hours of probing and questioning from a spouse confused by his or her mate's indirectness.

Steve struggled with this problem. He just couldn't express his thoughts without being vague about them. To avoid directly addressing a topic, he'd wander off the subject and talk about a score of other things. This was particularly true whenever the subject of finances came up. His wife wanted to know how much they could afford to spend on groceries in a given month. Steve *started* to talk about finances, but wound up drifting off into a discussion of the fascinating process used to print money. She never did get a straight answer from him about their financial situation—until a bill collector came to the door to repossess some of their furniture.

Some subjects can be difficult to talk about. But being indirect can increase, not decrease, potential problems. If your spouse has trouble being direct, ask yourself the following questions. Am I doing all I can to make it possible for him or her to open up? Do I let my spouse ignore issues that really ought to be talked about?

Perhaps we simply need to encourage our spouse to speak more directly. We should thank our mate when they *do* speak directly, rather than pouncing on them every time they don't. The Apostle John writes, "There is to be no fear in love; but perfect love casts out fear" (1 John 4:18). If you are fearful about speaking directly, just consider what the Bible teaches. We are never told to fear men, only God (Matt. 10:28). With His love as our strength, we can have the courage to speak about issues directly.

(5) *Couples should lock themselves into one way of communicating.* Do you remember Jim and Janet, the couple with very different spiritual backgrounds? They had another problem as well. They were locked into one way of communicating. Since Jim was the "teacher," he was under

the impression that *he* had to do the lion's share of talking. After all, he was supposed to be the "profound" one in this relationship. Yet there were times when Janet had important things to say. She often wished that Jim would just shut up for a minute and listen to her.

Open communication is meant to be enjoyed by both spouses, by people who are relating as friends and peers. But it cannot occur when we get tied into only one way of relating to each other.

To reverse this communication killer, take turns talking and listening; take turns being the "teacher" and the "student"; take turns being the initiator and the responder. At all costs, avoid getting locked into a way of communicating that's headed down a dead end street.

(6) *Don't worry about your tone of voice; after all, only your words are important.* I'm convinced that many of us simply do not realize how important the tone of our voice is to the success or failure of marital communication. In one counseling session, for instance, I listened to a wife whine on and on about her husband's various failings. When I mentioned to her that her voice had a rather moaning, complaining tone to it, she flatly denied my charge. When I further suggested that this tone might account for the reason her husband "tuned her out" so frequently, she became absolutely livid.

Since I tape record my counseling sessions—so couples can later review what we've discussed—I replayed the last few minutes of our session for this woman. For the first time, she heard how unpleasant her pleading tone sounded. Consequently, she resolved to speak with her spouse in a more direct, less emotional manner. This one change produced almost overnight improvements in their marriage.

Whether it be the rough edge of anger, the wearing sound of nagging, or the biting sting of sarcasm, we need to examine the way we sound to our spouse. To do so, let me encourage you to complete an assignment. This exercise can help you learn more about yourself, and hopefully, improve the way you come across to your spouse.

During the course of a week, turn on a tape recorder each evening. The first night, you may feel a little inhibited or uncomfortable talking with a tape rolling. But let a few nights go by, and you can gain a rather interesting picture of what your "normal" marital communication sounds like.

This idea may seem silly, but couples who've tried it report encouraging results. Often, they'll remark that listening to their own voices showed them why their marital communication was less than successful. They were unaware that they frequently used a nagging or condescending tone of voice in speaking with their spouse.

Remember, then, it's not merely *what* you say that's important, but *how* you say it.

(7) *Don't be concerned about things you say in anger; your spouse will forget what's been said.* As a child, did you ever recite the lines, "Sticks and stones may break my bones, but words will never hurt me"? I've got news for you: that little ditty is a lie. Words can devastate a spouse and destroy a marriage.

Many of my counselees tell me that words spoken to them in anger have troubled them for months. In most cases, the spouse who spoke the offending words doesn't even remember uttering them. But angry phrases have an unfortunate way of leaving a nasty, painful sting in the back of one's memory.

In light of these facts, I think we all can agree on at least one rule of healthy communication. We should say only those words we'd be glad to have our spouse remember. Words of love and caring never have to be apologized for. Yet words spoken in the heat of battle often will leave heart-wrenching scars—regardless of our attempts to retract them. Proverbs puts it this way: "A soothing tongue is a tree of life, but perversion in it crushes the spirit" (15:4).

We must recognize the impact of angry words. We're kidding ourselves if we think they don't have a killing impact on marriage.

PUTTING THINGS IN PERSPECTIVE

I hope that this look at communication squelchers hasn't left you depressed. Rather, it was my wish that they'd challenge you. Healthy communication isn't impossible—it just takes work!

On the next page, you'll find a summary of the principles we've studied so far. In this brief "communication creed," I've tried to present the lessons of this chapter in a helpful and handy manner. You might even want to photocopy this page and place it where you'll see it daily (the bathroom mirror, the refrigerator, etc.)

I hope this chapter has illustrated how working on communication skills with your spouse can reduce conflict and misunderstanding in your marriage. Practicing the fine art of communication is one of the most important things you can do to grow together!

COMMUNICATION CREED

Lord, You know that I want to be a better communicator. Remind me that You are the Author of communication. Throughout this week, as I look at these principles, help me to practice them with my mate. Keep me close to You, and draw me closer to my spouse. Remind me often that...

(1) I am always communicating—even when I think I'm hiding behind a wall of silence.

(2) Both my words and my nonverbal actions need to communicate the same message.

(3) A loving home environment offers the security my spouse needs to share his or her deepest feelings.

(4) I must not allow troublesome relationships outside my marriage to interfere with marital communication. I need to make such wrong relationships right.

(5) When I'm having a serious talk with my spouse, maintaining close physical contact between us is helpful.

(6) The gift of not interrupting my spouse is one that I owe to him or her.

(7) Even if it seems difficult, I will communicate with my mate in a clear and direct manner.

(8) Both my spouse and I are responsible for initiating communication.

(9) I need to keep tabs on my tone of voice.

(10) You can help me, God, to say words that my spouse will enjoy remembering.

EXERCISES IN GROWING TOGETHER

(1) Ask your spouse to describe a recent incident in which you stopped communicating *verbally*, but continued to convey a *nonverbal* message. Did you realize you were doing this at the time? What emotion were you trying to communicate through your nonverbal message?

_____

_____

_____

_____

(2) Ask your spouse what steps you can take to make him or her feel more secure about sharing personal emotions. You may be shocked by what you hear; perhaps you didn't know your mate feels ridiculed every time he or she opens up to you. Maybe you didn't realize you had a condescending tone. Be honest with one another—but also be loving!

_____

_____

_____

_____

(3) Tell your spouse several things he or she does that make for healthy conversation between you. Mention one thing he or she does that hinders effective communication.

_____

_____

_____

_____

(4) Of the seven "communication killers" listed in this

chapter, which ones do you find yourself using in your marriage? What specific steps can you take to reverse that behavior?

_____

_____

_____

_____

(5) Refer to the Marriage Enrichment Program in Chapter Eleven for further helpful information.

SEVEN

Conquering Conflict

Con•flict/ʹkan-flikt/ n (*conflictus*, act of striking together)
1. a fight, clash, contention. 2. sharp disagreement or oppo-
sition, as of interests, ideas, etc. 3. mutual interference of
incompatible forces or wills.

At first glance, the definition printed above seems to provide a comprehensive understanding of the term, "conflict."
But if you stop to think about it, the impact of conflict on
marriage cannot be reduced to a neat, sterilized dictionary
entry. The volumes of hurt written in the hearts of couples
ravaged by conflict go beyond mere words. Couples who've
experienced conflict aren't really interested in precise defi-
nitions, anyway. They're looking for answers.

Can anything positive come out of conflict? Is there any
way to replace emotional mayhem with reasonable solutions? Can we prevent disagreements from destroying the
trust on which marriage is built? As with our study of
communication, a single chapter cannot hope to answer
every question couples have about conflict. But it *is* possible to shine some light on ways husbands and wives can
cope with conflict. In the words of Isaiah, couples *can* learn
to "come ... and reason together" (1:18).

I know what some couples are saying right now. "Conflict? We *never* have conflict in our relationship." Well, if you're a reader who's only been married a week, perhaps you *haven't* ever experienced conflict with your spouse. But if you're like the rest of us, I suggest you stick around. For those of us who occasionally lace up the gloves and go at it, let's learn how to soften our blows. Let's learn how to harness the emotional energy we'd otherwise expend on fighting, and start growing together.

WHY DO WE FIGHT?
As we learn how to deal with friction in marriage, we first need to answer a fundamental question. Why do couples argue?

From a biblical perspective, we can identify one basic factor which interrupts marital bliss: sin. In his excellent book *The Trauma of Transparency*, Grant Howard takes us on a tour of the Garden of Eden. He points out that once Satan planted the seeds of pride, selfishness, and defensiveness in that once-beautiful garden, it did not take long for conflict to infest human relationships. And as descendants of Adam and Eve, each of us has inherited two of their attributes: the abilities to "hide" and "hurl" (Multnomah Press, pp. 47-68). We fear being rejected, so we "hide" behind emotional masks—just as Adam tried to hide in the Garden (Gen. 3:8). We can't stand being told we're wrong, so we learn to "hurl" back angry words—just as Adam blamed Eve (3:12).

Our own sin, then, is the underlying reason that conflict crops up in a relationship. It's an inescapable fact: we are imperfect, sinful people. We all are bent on having our own way. When pushed to do something we'd rather not, or when we're told we've done something wrong, defensiveness comes quicky to the surface. And if we look closely at how sin manifests itself in marital relationships, we can see a peculiar function it plays—a function that feeds off our natural tendency to "hide" and "hurl."

THE FUNCTION OF FRICTION

For years, Gary and Debbie had enjoyed a happy marriage. Oh, they had the usual problems—sick kids, bills to pay. But they also spent a great deal of time with one another. Vacations, trips to the zoo, and quiet dinners all were parts of their marriage. Yet when Gary accepted a promotion at work, these features began to disappear.

Gary's new position required him to spend a considerable amount of time at the office. With her husband gone so much, nearly all the parenting responsibilities fell to Debbie. At first she didn't mind this arrangement. But then she began to feel unsupported and overwhelmed by the children. She asked Gary to be more involved at home, but he always had justifiable reasons why he could not. Work, you know.

Soon, Debbie found herself growing increasingly irritable. Always a rather tolerant mother, she now started to take out her frustrations over this new domestic situation on her children. She drew up a list of stringent rules. The kids' rooms not only had to be clean, they had to be spotless. Toys could not be left out under any circumstance. Clothes always had to be hung up.

The children initially complied with these new demands. But soon, their attitude toward their mother shifted to one of disrespect. One night, a heated argument broke out between Debbie and the children. Gary, who had just gotten home from work and was relaxing in front of the TV, finally had to intervene in this shouting match to restore some peace and quiet.

After that initial confrontation, mother/children battles erupted almost every night. Inevitably, Gary was called in to settle these fights. And as these battles continued, Gary and Debbie became more and more angry with *one another*. Gary was mad that Debbie couldn't handle the children better; Debbie was angry that Gary had become little more than a disciplinarian. Now, the least little thing set off an argument between them.

What could this couple have done to reverse this slide? For one, they should have recognized *why* they were fighting. Basically, by arguing with one another, each partner was trying to change the other's behavior. Debbie wanted more help from her husband; Gary wanted his wife to understand his need to unwind at the end of a long day without interruption.

Why do we fight? One answer lies in the *function* of conflict. By arguing, we are trying to *achieve* something. The next time you and your spouse disagree, ask yourself the following questions. What's the purpose of this argument? What am I trying to achieve through it? Am I arguing to get my own way, to change my spouse's behavior, to establish new modes of relating, to hurt my mate's feelings?

I still can remember the look on Debbie and Gary's face when I first asked them what function they thought their conflict was performing. Neither of them really had thought of conflict in this sense. Later, they were able to come to grips with this concept. They were able to see that they were fighting in order to produce changes in their roles as parents and spouses. Once they understood the function of friction, they were able to rebuild their relationship.

The starting place for dealing with disagreements comes with recognizing that we are sinful people. Then we must realize that we argue because we are trying to achieve certain goals. Disagreements *will* come to all married couples. But the answer is not to wish them away; we must acknowledge the role they play, and work at learning skills to overcome them.

As for this last point, let's now turn our attention to six helpful ways of dealing with conflict. Each of these guidelines can teach us how to respond to one another in love, rather than anger.

CONFLICT AS A LIFE-SAVING SIGNAL

For centuries, both Christians and non-Christians have struggled with the problem of pain. Why does it occur? How can we avoid it? If someone offered us a pill that could keep us from feeling pain, most of us probably would jump at the opportunity to take it. But *should* we?

The dread disease of leprosy provides a graphic example of what happens when people *can't* feel pain. As I understand it, leprosy can cause the body's pain receptors to cease functioning properly. Thus, lepers cannot feel pressures or temperatures that would make other people flinch.

While this may sound like a blessing, it actually is a curse. The body's inability to feel pain allows unnoticed irritants to cause irreparable damage. Stories have been reported of lepers who've lost an arm or leg when these limbs came too close to an open fire. The absence of the life-saving signal of pain prevented the leper from realizing what was happening to the limb.

How does all this relate to couples who are experiencing confict? Marriage counselors generally agree that couples who are extremely angry with one another are *not* the most difficult type of people to work with. It is the couple who is emotionally numb, the couple who *never* fights, that's hard to counsel. When a couple no longer feels any pain or pleasure, when they have moved so far apart that one partner's actions fail to produce a reaction from the other— then the red flags go up. It is difficult to bring about changes in the face of emotional deadness.

That's why in marriage, as with the human body, pain can provide people with a life-saving signal. It can serve to point out a couple's need to reexamine and work at their relationship.

I once heard a lecture by a man who actually looked forward to times of marital tension. David Mace is well-respected in both Christian and secular circles for his work in marriage counseling. While his professional credentials certainly are impressive, what impresses me *more* about this man is the fact that he has been married to the same woman for over fifty years. Now that's practicing what you preach!

After fifty years of marriage, and with all his training in marriage enrichment and counseling, I expected him to report that his marriage was conflict-free. But he told us, "After all these years of marriage, my wife and I never miss an opportunity to argue." Why would he say that?

David and Vera Mace have learned that painful disagreements can expose problems in their relationship that need to be worked out. Suppose they argue over whether to purchase a new car. This disagreement might really indicate that they have deep-seated differences over how one should handle money. Obviously, for a marriage to grow, such differences must be resolved.

Pain *does* have a way of grabbing our attention. And this wise couple has learned the simple lesson that painful situations can be "used" to improve their relationship.

James records a similar thought in his epistle: "Consider it all joy, my brethren, when you encounter various trials, knowing that the testing of your faith produces endurance" (1:2-3). Like it or not, trials are one way God deepens and strengthens our faith. Marital trials can offer us a similar opportunity. We can learn more about each other—and about trusting God—as we work through our disagreements and grow together.

This first guideline should challenge couples to look at marital disagreements as opportunities for growth, not as obstacles to it. Pain can show us how to deepen our marriage—if we don't ignore its life-saving signal.

DO YOU WANT TO FACE FOXES OR LIONS?
When it comes to repairing my car, I live by the motto, "Why fix the squeak today that might go away by itself tomorrow." I hate to admit it, but this cavalier attitude has led to two major overhauls I could have avoided.

Ignoring funny noises in a car is one thing. But when squeaks start developing in a marital relationship, it's important to take notice. They may indicate that a problem needs our attention.

This second guideline for growing together through conflict is wonderfully pictured in the Song of Solomon. Here, Solomon's bride asks him early in their marriage to attend to small problems before they get out of hand. In poetic fashion, she asks her husband to:

Catch the foxes for us, the little foxes that are ruining
the vineyards, while our vineyards are in blossom
(2:15).

This bride knew that if seemingly small annoyances were allowed to run free, they could result in significant damage to their relationship. For modern-day couples, "small" problems like procrastinating on projects around the house, slipping into a habit of sarcasm, or forgetting about manners at the dinner table can snowball quickly. Before a couple realizes it, a "fox" has turned into an emotional "lion."

Why not get into a habit of asking your spouse, "Are we keeping 'short accounts'? Are we resolving small problems quickly?" These types of questions provide an opportunity for couples to deal with small issues before they escalate into major problems. Couples who learn to keep "short accounts" will do a far better job of capturing foxes. After all, who wants to wrestle a lion?

TAKE TURNS GETTING ANGRY

A third guideline for containing conflict may seem rather difficult to follow; yet it can dramatically keep arguments from running out of control.

Basically, I advise spouses to "take turns" getting angry. Let me try to illustrate what I mean.

In Dallas, where my wife and I lived for some time, there's a stretch of freeway know as Central Expressway. This strip of asphalt is a race-car driver's dream. Cars can go from zero to sixty on it in a matter of seconds.

Cindy and I frequently traveled together on the Central

Expressway and I must confess, I always enjoyed the thrill of racing along on it. However, my predilection for driving in the "Commuter 500" was driving Cindy to distraction. She simply was not accustomed to huge freeways; and she certainly wasn't used to riding with an aspiring Grand Prix driver.

One day things finally boiled over. I was following close behind another car, when it suddenly braked to a stop. Our car came safely to the halt, though for a moment, I thought my wife and I were going to wind up in the other guy's backseat. Gripping the handle on the dashboard and stomping on an imaginary brake, Cindy exploded in anger. She wanted to get off the freeway—*now!*

"Get off the freeway?" I bellowed. "Not a chance!" After all, I was a seasoned freeway driver. My wife would just have to get used to driving in the big city. And if she wanted to be angry with me, fine! I'd be angry right back!

Later that evening, when the smoke finally cleared, Cindy told me about a terrible automobile accident she had been in as a young girl. My driving had ignited all those old fears. Out on the expressway, I had been unwilling to listen to her legitimate concerns. I was too busy being angry at her for being angry at me to understand the source of it.

This example illustrates why I encourage couples to "take turns" being angry. When both people get caught up in the anger of the moment—as Cindy and I did—genuine problems can be ignored.

In counseling, I tell couples that anger is a *secondary*, not a *primary* emotion. This means that the emotion of anger usually is tied to some other feeling. As a teenager, did you ever promise your parents that you'd be home by 10 o'clock—and then not show up until long after midnight? Because of their love for you, your parents were concerned. Because they feared for your safety, they called the local hospital a half dozen times to see if you'd been in an accident.

But once you *did* get home, they *weren't* waiting for you

with a warm reception. They probably were ready to warm a certain portion of your anatomy. But we understood why our parents reacted this way. We realized that behind their frowns, they were worried and concerned about us.

Many couples lack this kind of discernment. When a spouse gets angry, we're more apt to return his or her outburst, than we are to look for the reasons behind it. Yet if we concentrate all our energy on matching our mate's angry behavior, we'll never get anywhere. We need to employ a stop/think approach to disagreements; we ought to stay calm and consider *what's* motivating our spouse's outburst. Then we can try to respond to his or her anger in healthy ways.

When you think about it, it's hard for a person to continue an argument when the other person refuses to fight back. Staying in control when our mate is irate goes against our natural grain. But it's a godly response to make:

> He who is slow to anger is better than the mighty. And he who rules his spirit, than he who captures a city (Prov 16:32).

FOCUS ON THE PROBLEM, NOT THE PERSON
A fourth guideline for constructive problem-solving involves keeping our guns aimed at our problems, rather than our spouse. Follow this typical chain of events.

Keith and Karen disagree over how to spend an unexpected gift of money. Keith wants to spend it on a new stereo and some yard equipment. Karen wants to keep it in the bank for a rainy day. As long as they continue to focus on the *issue* of how the money will be spent or saved, they're well on their way to solving this problem.

But let's say that Keith and Karen refuse to change their positions on this matter. Keith wants to spend; Karen wants to save. Neither one is willing to budge an inch. If they're not careful, they could begin to attack *one another*, instead of the problem.

If this happened, we'd begin to hear them say things such as, "Any *considerate* husband would . . . " or, "If you were a *submissive* wife, you'd. . . . " Now shots are being fired at a spouse, rather than the issue. Instead of deciding what to do with the money, Keith and Karen have gotten caught up in criticizing one another.

If this behavior continues, their conflict will move up one more notch: now they'll begin to question the wisdom of continuing their *relationship*. At this level, we might hear Keith say, "If that's the kind of person you are, maybe I never should have married you." Not to be outdone, Karen can come right back with, "My old boyfriend, Marty, was always willing to compromise. Maybe I should have married *him!*"

Couples interested in growing together must learn to keep their arguments on the ground floor—at the *issue* level. At this level, a couple is focusing on the problem itself and is attempting to find ways to solve it. Yet some couples don't contain conflict at this stage. They move up a level and begin to attack their partner, or scale the heights and start questioning their relationship. The more time a couple spends at level two (attacking the person), or at level three (questioning the relationship), the more easily a marriage can be torn apart.

Ask yourself a difficult question. What level do you stop at in disagreeing with your spouse? Better yet, ask your wife or husband what level *he* or *she* thinks you stop at. Just remember: we can solve more misunderstandings when we attack our problems, than when we assault our life's partner.

LAUGHTER: THE BEST MEDICINE

Can laughter save your life? Well, several recent studies have shown it's actually *healthy* to laugh. Some physicians, in fact, believe that sick people literally can "laugh themselves well." Take the case of Norman Cousins.

Best-selling author Cousins was told he had an incurable,

fatal illness. But he wasn't willing to give up without a fight. Instead of moaning over his condition, Cousins had old comedy movies brought into his room. For hours on end, he laughed as he watched the antics of Laurel and Hardy or Charlie Chaplin. What happened? Cousins made a miraculous recovery. He attributes it, in part, to the recuperative power of laughter.

Right about now, some of you probably are saying, "That's a nice story, Trent, but there's nothing funny about the arguments going on in our house." I'm sure there isn't. But perhaps it's time you took a dose of humor to rescue a critically ill marriage.

I once knew a husband and wife who really wanted their marriage to work. But they just couldn't seem to stop arguing. They spent weeks in counseling with me. We went over scores of problems. And still they argued.

Do you know what finally broke their cycle of constant arguing? That's right: humor.

In a graduate class I was taking at the time, we were studying the use of humor as a tension-relieving device. Frankly, I had run out of ideas to keep this particular couple from arguing, so I decided to give humor a try.

I gave them a simple assignment. Straight-faced, I told them to leave my office, drive directly to the local convenience store, and buy two squirt guns. Then, the next time an argument started, they were to fill the guns with water and begin shooting at each other.

The assignment worked perfectly! For the first time in months, this couple actually laughed together. They found it impossible to argue and squirt one another at the same time. Humor brought relief and a new willingness to improve their marriage.

My wife puts this principle into practice in our home. If the tone of my voice becomes angry or sarcastic, she'll begin to quack like a duck! I know it sounds crazy, but it makes both of us laugh and really helps me watch my tone of voice.

This may be the first time someone has encouraged you to inject humor into a serious moment. But don't brush this guideline aside. It could help turn a tense moment into a constructive one.

THE IMPORTANCE OF PLANNING

This final guideline for dealing with conflict involves the importance of advanced planning. All too often, couples just sit and stew or "stand back and let it fly" when it comes to discussing their problems. It's much more helpful to work through difficulties in an organized fashion. And for that, you need a plan.

Do you remember Keith and Karen, the couple we met a few pages ago? As they tried to decide what to do with their unexpected money, they let their discussion get away from them. They couldn't agree with one another, so they began to tear their relationship apart.

What they needed was a discussion plan—a plan that could guide the course of their conversation, help them understand their feelings, and lead them to a healthy decision. Such a plan has several parts.

First, Keith and Karen should agree to follow four rules even *before* their discussion begins.

(1) *They should set up a specific time to talk through their problem.* Unfortunately, many couples put off talking with one another, claiming they must "mow the lawn" or "give the kids a bath" first. Therefore, Keith and Karen should pick a time when all these things are finished, when outside distractions are at a minimum. That way they can be guaranteed a time of uninterrupted conversation.

(2) *After they have set the time, they should keep it.* There's nothing worse than a "no show." Let's say that Keith has agreed to talk about this problem "as soon as the basketball game is over." Once the game ends, he should not plead for time to watch "just one more show"; if he does, his credibility as an honest, trustworthy spouse will plummet. Keith should give Karen the same respect he

would any other important appointment.

(3) *They should address only one issue at a time.* If Keith and Karen try to solve every problem confronting their relationship in just one sitting, it's a sure bet that *none* of their problems will get resolved. Given the complex nature of most marital disagreements, couples can't expect to clear the slate in one fell swoop. Each problem needs to be addressed individually, sensitively. Consequently, even if it takes fifteen separate meetings to set their marriage straight, Keith and Karen should stick to discussing only the money problem at this time.

(4) *They should agree only to use edifying words with one another.* In short, yelling, name-calling, and hair-pulling are *not* to be a part of discussion times. In fact, Keith and Karen should start their talk by saying at least one positive, reaffirming thing about the other. Then they can get into discussing their problem.

With these preliminary rules in place, Keith and Karen now are ready to discuss this important money matter. This doesn't have to be a marathon discussion. Cindy and I often have accomplished more in a short talk than in dialogues that ran far into the night. In Keith and Karen's case, they have set a limit of one hour in which to decide how the money will be allocated.

If Karen was the spouse who called for this little talk, she should initiate a three-step discussion plan.

(1) *Karen should concisely explain her concern to Keith.* Karen might say, "I'm concerned about what we should do with this money. I'm afraid we'll just go out and spend it all without leaving any for savings." Keith then should restate Karen's concern as he understands it. He might say, for example, "You're concerned that all the money we received will be spent, whereas saving it might be wiser." Such a response indicates that Keith understands the essence of Karen's concern. Karen would tell him that he is correct, and they could proceed to step two.

But if Keith were to say, "As *usual*, you're *never* satisfied with what we have in savings. You *never* want to buy anything I want to," it would be clear that he was responding in an emotional and inaccurate manner. In that case, Karen would need to repeat her concern. Once Karen was sure Keith understood her, they could proceed to step two.

(2) *Karen should use an emotional word picture to try to explain her feelings about this issue.* It's often been said that one picture is worth a thousand words. This also is true when it comes to using "emotional word pictures"—brief, symbolic phrases which describe a person's *feelings* on a given matter.

In "painting" such a "picture," Karen might say, "When we spend large amounts of money, I feel as though I'm walking on a sidewalk covered with ice."

As in step one above, Keith should restate her word picture and explain what he thinks she's trying to say through it. Since Keith grew up in Chicago, he knows what it's like to walk on a slippery, icy sidewalk. It gives one a feeling of uncertainty and insecurity. At any moment, you can fall and hurt yourself. Karen's word picture reflects how a small savings balance makes her feel. It diminishes her sense of financial security—it makes her feel as though she's walking on ice.

If Keith accurately interprets this picture, the couple now is able to move to the final step.

(3) *Karen should suggest a workable solution to this problem.* At this point in the discussion process, Keith and Karen are not making any ironclad agreements. They're simply discussing possible solutions. But Karen should use this opportunity to share her perspective on how the money ought to be handled. Let's imagine she says, "I'd like to place two thirds of the money in savings, and spend one third on the purchase of a stereo." As with the steps outlined above, Keith should restate Karen's suggestion to make sure it was not misconstrued.

After this is accomplished, Keith and Karen should trade places. In other words, Keith should go back to step one and express *his* concerns. Then he should share his feelings in an emotional word picture, and finally, present his solution to their problem. In each case, Karen should restate what she has heard her husband say.

When both Keith and Karen have finished sharing their problems, feelings, and solutions, they should wrap things up by answering the following three questions.

(1) Of the solutions discussed, which one would be the best for our *relationship*—rather than for any one person? Can we choose a solution where neither of us loses?

(2) Do either of us need to ask the other's forgiveness? Were either of us overly emotional or angry before or during our discussion?

(3) Finally, do we both feel comfortable with and committed to the decision we made before the Lord? If one person has had to make a major concession, do any feelings still need to be talked out?

We've looked at six ways to grow through conflict. Each of them can help you harness the energy that's expended during a disagreement and turn it into a positive force. Why not ask the Lord today to help you put these problem-solving skills to work? They can make even the most difficult times an opportunity for growing together!

EXERCISES IN GROWING TOGETHER

(1) Think about a recent argument you've had with your spouse. What marriage-saving "signal" might it have been sending you? What area(s) of your marriage might your fight have indicated needed improvement?

_____

_____

_____

_____

(2) Do you keep "short accounts" with your mate; that is, do you resolve problems as soon as they arise, or do you let them stew? Are there any problems or issues you've been mulling over for months, but have yet to discuss with your spouse? Take this time to bring these problems out into the open. You owe it to your marriage to do so.

_____

_____

_____

_____

(3) If it's important to "take turns" getting angry, what specific steps can you and your spouse take to ensure that one of you stays calm during an argument? Obviously, this is not an easy task; but seek to be creative.

_____

_____

_____

_____

(4) Practice the problem-solving plan presented at the end of this chapter. Pick an issue that needs to be talked through, then follow the pattern outlined here. Did discussing an issue this way differ from the way you usually

resolve problems? Was it more effective?

_____

_____

_____

_____

(5) Refer to the Marriage Enrichment Program in Chapter Eleven for further helpful information.

EIGHT

"Drink Deeply, O Lovers"

Our society is very confused. Few people would disagree with so broad a statement, so let's narrow our focus a bit. Try this on for size: Our society is very confused *about sex.* Just consider a few of the new and conflicting theories that have been spewn forth to explain how you and I can reach the pinnacle of sexual satisfaction.

Some books, with titles such as *Men Are Just Desserts* and *Nice Girls Do and So Should You,* speak of the need for women to unshackle themselves from "puritanical" restraints and become "sexually free." *Shared Intimacies* and *The Cohabitation Handbook* tell us that switching sexual partners will provide the basis for fulfillment. And in *The Joy of Gay Sex,* homosexual relationships are promoted as an acceptable alternative to God's design for "one man, one woman."

These books all claim to hold the key to sexual fulfillment. Yet like salty popcorn, they promise refreshment—but only produce an unquenchable thirst. If we look to our society for a definition of what constitutes a satisfying sexual relationship, we'll be caught in a house of mirrors. What appears to be a fulfilling alternative today will be twisted and distorted tomorrow.

More than ever, we need a message that will cut through the sexual confusion clouding our society. In essence, I believe we need to listen to the Creator of sex if we are to find our way through this maze and discover true physical fulfillment. Only then will we learn to grow together in this most treasured of areas.

THE PROBLEM WITH
"DOING WHAT COMES NATURALLY"

Some people simply don't believe that one's sex life should be placed under the lordship of Christ. Once, after speaking on this topic at a conference, a couple came up to me.

"Now don't get me wrong," the husband said. "I think that what God has to say about sex is important. But wouldn't it be better if we forget all this talk and just started doing what comes naturally?"

Doing what comes naturally. That sure sounds like a great way to live. "Natural" cereals and "natural" hair products are the current rage. Perhaps the key to a satisfying sexual relationship simply involves being "natural" too. I'm sure that being "natural" worked for Adam and Eve in the Garden. In this beautiful setting, separated from sin and the perversions of our society, "The man and his wife were both naked and were not ashamed" (Gen. 2:25).

But in a sinful world, following our "natural" inclinations no longer can guarantee that our needs—sexual or otherwise—will be fulfilled. Sin has obscured our ability to faultlessly determine what's "good" for us. We need, therefore, to listen to God's instructions if we are to find true satisfaction. Why? Because there is a marked contrast between the value of worldly counsel and the timeless Word of God.

Our culture says, "Women are no different from men." Our Lord says they were created very differently in terms of their emotional and physical makeup (1 Peter 3:7).

Our culture says, "commitment" to one person kills a healthy sex life. Our Lord says commitment is the only foundation on which it will grow (Gen. 2:24).

Our culture says, "Premarital sex can't be wrong if it feels so right." Our Lord says we are to be controlled by His Spirit, not our glands (Gal. 5:1).

Our culture says, "guilt" is a thing of the past. Our Lord offers true forgiveness to those who otherwise would never be able to forget the past (2 Cor. 5:17).

And when it comes to solving problems that affect all marriages, His Word is more valuable than any "natural" perception (Ps. 19:10). Take a moment to study the diagram on the next page. It outlines several factors that can adversely influence a couple's sexual life. After we examine each of these potential problems, we'll consider how a relationship with the living God can make a difference in solving them.

THE LAYERS OF LIFE

Physical desires are nothing to be ashamed of. In fact, they're mentioned in the Song of Solomon, the Bible's picture of marital love. At the very outset of this book, Solomon's bride says: "May he kiss me with the kisses of his mouth!" (1:2) Obviously, this couple was strongly attracted to one another!

Many couples begin their marriage with these same strong drives and desires. Yet after the honeymoon, their sexual relationship seems to lose much of its spark. Why is that? In many cases, a number of intervening factors—or, as I call them, "layers of life"—make it difficult for couples to experience a sexually fulfilling relationship.

If the "perfect" marriage existed, a couple's sexual desires would flow unhindered into a beautiful physical union, despite life's difficulties and concerns. But, again, since we live in an imperfect world, our desires inevitably flow through, or are affected by, these "layers." "Layers" include:

Physical differences. Often, spouses simply are unaware of the role physical differences can play in a marriage. For example, the time it takes to sexually arouse one's partner usually differs considerably between men and women; a

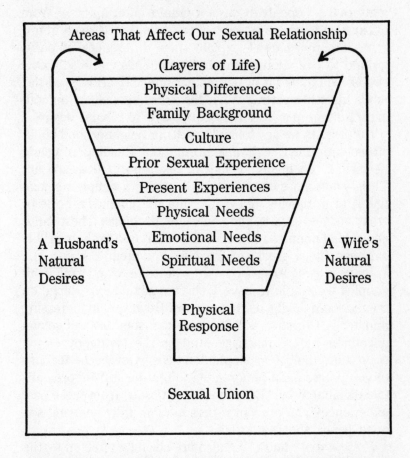

Areas That Affect Our Sexual Relationship

(Layers of Life)

Physical Differences

Family Background

Culture

Prior Sexual Experience

Present Experiences

Physical Needs

Emotional Needs

Spiritual Needs

A Husband's Natural Desires

A Wife's Natural Desires

Physical Response

Sexual Union

husband can become aroused in ninety *seconds*, whereas the average wife takes between twenty and thirty *minutes* before she becomes fully aroused (Neil Carlson, *The Physiology of Behavior*, Allyn and Bacon, p. 331). I'm sure you can imagine the problems caused by a husband who rushes into the sexual act simply because *he's* ready: his wife is left unfulfilled and decidedly unexcited. If this pattern persists, sexual desire on the part of both spouses can decline.

Family background. While few people learn about sex directly from their parents, couples still are greatly influenced by their family's attitudes and actions toward sex. For example, some people come from a home where sexual matters were openly discussed. Others enter marriage from backgrounds where sex rarely was mentioned, even in private. If couples don't explain their differences in background to one another, misunderstandings can result. One spouse will think his or her mate is unnecessarily "prudish," while the other partner views his or her spouse as "immodest." Neither perception is conducive to sexual desire.

Culture. As we've already noted, our neighborhood bookstores are filled with misinformation. Reading romantic bestsellers or highly technical sex reports that are not Christ-centered can confuse and hinder a couple's sexual life. Add in movies, television, and the media's reports of what "normal" sex is, and you've got problems. These influences lead couples to believe that everyone in the world is experiencing a great sex life—except them!

Prior sexual experience. It would be wonderful if all couples were able to have their first sexual experience on their wedding night, as God intends. However, an increasing number of Christian couples have had some sort of sexual encounter before marriage. And as the testimony of my counselees indicates, people don't easily forget the feelings of guilt, regret, and remorse that often result from premarital sexual activity. "Emotional scar tissue" from these past experiences can prevent a person from fully enjoying sex once he or she is married.

Present experience. We also are strongly affected by the present. A "hard day at the office" or a "rough time with the kids" can reduce a person's capacity to feel caring or loving toward a spouse; studies have shown that sexual desire goes down as stress goes up. If our body is busy fighting stress, it's easy for pleasurable feelings to be drained away.

Physical and emotional needs. Certain needs can act like a sponge in soaking up sexual desire. A long-term illness or emotional problem can severely influence sexual desire. If our spouse is in physical or emotional pain, it is clear we can expect a marked reduction in his or her interest in sex.

Spiritual needs. Problems in this area can be the most

destructive of all. If our relationship is not right with the Lord, we should expect other areas of life to be out of balance too. That is why couples who lose their desire to pray together often lose their sexual desire for one another. The inability to pray with one's spouse usually is symptomatic of a larger disease: spiritual apathy. No aspect of the marriage relationship (including sex) is spared from apathy's ravenous onslaught.

Each of these "layers of life" can affect a husband's or wife's sexual desire. How well we physically respond to our mate, then, is a product of how clear or cluttered these "layers" are. If there are no clogging elements to drain away sexual desire, a couple can respond to one another in satisfying ways. But if one or more "layers" are blocked or obstructed, a married couple's physical relationship will suffer. Impotence, for example, often is due to a persistent emotional problem in a person's life—or, to use our analogy, a continuously "blocked level."

Obviously, this is not what God desires.

SIX NOURISHING PRINCIPLES

A satisfying sexual relationship begins when the God of creation makes each "layer of life" clean and uncluttered. This "cleaning" process can begin when we choose to follow certain godly teachings.

Each of the six principles we'll study in the following pages come right from the Scriptures. While Christians have long been silent when it comes to talking about sexual matters, God is perfectly willing to address this subject in a straightforward manner.

The place of pleasure. Some couples I've counseled have wondered aloud whether God really approves of sex. In some cases, they've heard other Christians claim that sex is a result of man's fall from grace in the Garden. As such, sex is a necessary vehicle for procreation, but it is not intended for pleasure.

This attitude toward sex in marriage is not biblical. Hugh

Hefner wasn't the first person to come up with the idea that sex is something to be enjoyed. The Lord, Himself, designed marital love to be enjoyable and fully enjoyed. This is clearly seen in the Song of Solomon. In chapters four and five of this beautiful song of love, we're provided a glimpse of the couple's wedding night.

The scene is beautiful. After the royal wedding, all the guests have gone home. Alone at last on their first night as a married couple, bride and groom share the wonder and privilege of joining together sexually. They "eat" and "drink" of each aspect of love's feast.

Solomon speaks to his bride:

> I have come into my garden, my sister, my bride; I have gathered my myrrh along with my balsam. I have eaten my honeycomb and my honey; I have drunk my wine and my milk (5:1).

In sensitive, symbolic terms, Solomon tells us that he and his wife enjoyed every aspect of the sexual act. In fact, it reminded him of fragrant spices and the sweetest honey.

Then, a voice speaks to the couple:

> Eat, friends; drink and imbibe deeply, O Lovers (5:1).

To whom does this voice belong? Who is speaking at this point? Is it an uninvited guest? Is it a chorus of women who appeared earlier in the book? Certainly, neither of these intruders would be present in the bedroom on a couple's wedding night. Who is it, then, that speaks? Who is it that calls this couple to "Drink and imbibe deeply" of love's feast?

One writer notes:

> In the final analysis this must be the voice of the Creator, the greatest Poet, the most intimate wedding guest of all. The One who indeed prepared this lovely couple for the night of

His design. He lifts His voice and gives hearty approval to the entire night. He vigorously endorses and affirms the love of this couple. He takes pleasure in what has taken place. Two of His own have experienced love in all the beauty and fervor and purity that He intended for them. (S. Craig Glickman, *A Song for Lovers*, IVP, p. 25).

God was present on that wedding night, and on every night that followed. It is He who gave this couple the permission to enjoy the pleasures of the sexual act.

We should not chain ourselves to restrictive attitudes about sex which the Lord, Himself, does not promote. Freedom and excitement await any couple who will heed their Creator's call to "Eat, friends; drink and imbibe deeply, O Lovers."

A purified character promotes passion. Do you remember the opening words of the Song of Solomon, the ones we shared earlier? Solomon's bride says, "May he kiss me with the kisses of his mouth!" What husband wouldn't want his wife to say those same words! But did you ever wonder what *prompted* these feelings of passion? It was not an expensive cologne, but Solomon's personal *character* that produced an exciting fragrance for his wife. We read in the next verse, "Your oils have a pleasing fragrance, your *name* is like purified oil" (1:3; italics mine).

Solomon's bride points out a principle for increasing passion that we all ought to grasp: The more purified our character, the more attractive we will become to our spouse.

In Old Testament times, a person's name stood for much more than it does today. In fact, an individual's name represented all that person was or would become. This is why the Lord changed Abram's name to Abraham, "Father of nations." This is why He changed Jacob's name, which meant "grabber," to Israel.

Here in the Song of Solomon, this loving bride points out the source of her passion. Certainly, she thought

Solomon handsome; but she was even more attracted to his character. She says his name is like "purified oil." But what does that image have to do with his character?

In Israel, you still can see how people go about the process of "purifying" oil. A series of trays are stacked, one on top of the other. Each tray has different sized rocks in it, from large stones, down to fine pebbles. Oil is poured from the top tray through each successive layer. By the time the oil collects at the bottom, the impurities that once were a part of this liquid have been filtered out.

Solomon's life reflected this same process. His life had been filtered by trials and was free of rough edges. As he responded to tests and trials through God's wisdom, these events acted as purifying agents in his life.

This principle needs to be applied to contemporary marriages. If our lives are rough and filled with the impurities of a sin-stained life, we are not going to be an attractive sexual partner. If a wife constantly has to lie for her husband and cover up his business dealings, her passion level will drop dramatically. If a husband is subjected to his wife's bitter complaints, his sexual interest will decline, as well.

It may take trials to rub off the rough edges in our life, but a godly lifestyle is the best way to attract our spouse's passionate feelings. From God's perspective, passion will increase in a marriage if we concentrate on developing a righteous character.

The hazards of chasing the national average. I've often heard it said that we live in a culture which strives after excellence. We want to be the best at everything we do. I'm not so sure that's really true. Actually, I suspect that most of us struggle to be "average." For example, if we make "less than the average" salary, or spend more on groceries than the "average" family, we wonder where we've gone wrong!

Unfortunately, many couples also struggle to keep up with what they believe is "average" in the area of sex. They're more concerned with reading reports about what the "average" American's sex life is like, than they are with enjoying the physical aspects of their own marriage.

How should couples interpret the figures supplied in such reports? Frankly, I recommend they don't even bother with them! Keeping on par with national averages will not, in itself, produce sexual satisfaction. In day to day life, there always will be periods of high sexual activity, and periods when little activity occurs. Couples, therefore, must find what's "right" for them.

Actually, if we want to find the "right" level of sexual intimacy in our marriage, we should turn to Scripture for instruction:

> Let the husband fulfill his duty to his wife, and likewise also the wife to her husband. The wife does not have authority over her own body, but the husband does; and likewise also the husband does not have authority over his own body, but the wife does (1 Cor. 7:3-5).

In other words, a desire to respond to one another in love and to meet one another's needs, is the best guideline in deciding how and when to be intimate. Chasing a national average is a barrier, not a breakthrough, to a healthy sexual relationship. While a regular pattern of sexual contact is desirable, no tables or charts need dictate a loving couple's actions.

Focus on creative caring. In a relationship filled with the pressures and demands of daily life, we sometimes forget about our spouse's need to be cared for, to be treated tenderly. In some cases, we exhibit tenderness toward our mate only when we're in the mood for sex. Take, for example, the husband who is rough and unreachable most of the week. He growls every time he's asked to perform some minor task. Then, when Saturday night rolls around, he turns tender just when it's time to go to bed. How convenient! But this sort of "tenderness" usually doesn't communicate love; more than likely, his wife will wind up feeling exploited.

So how can a couple create a climate in which each person demonstrates tenderness and caring on a daily basis? How can a couple create a climate that will enhance their growth together in this vital area? Why not try the following practical exercise.

In counseling, I often have couples write out what Dr. Richard Stuart calls a "Caring Days" list (*Helping Couples Change*, Guilford Press, p. 192). This is a list of small, positive things you'd want your spouse to do for you— things that say, "I love you." It can include such requests as having a spouse say "thank you" for a meal, helping you with the dishes, lingering to give you a backrub, or taking your turn to bathe the children.

Once a spouse draws up this list, his or her mate is to select at least four items off it. There may be twelve possibilities to choose from, but the spouse must commit him or herself to doing these four during the next week without being asked.

It's been my experience that when small acts of caring are a regular part of a marriage, significant changes take place in a couple's sexual relationship. In addition to rekindling a couple's feelings of love, these "caring actions" can fan the flames of sexual desire. In the Song of Solomon's seven short chapters, Solomon demonstrates tenderness toward his bride by praising her over fifty times! Since we've already seen that their marriage was a passionate one, it would seem safe to conclude that a direct link exists between communicating to our spouse in a caring manner, and sexual fulfillment.

Don't be afraid to ask questions. My first day in Hebrew class during seminary was an anxious event. Just figuring out how the letters of the alphabet were supposed to look "right side up" turned out to be a problem for me. While I didn't want to appear ignorant in front of my classmates, I also didn't want to fall hopelessly behind.

Fortunately, my professor knew how to defuse a tense situation. He began the class by stating, "Men, I want you to know that the only 'dumb' question, is the unasked question." Swallowing my pride, I went ahead and asked my questions. Having the freedom to ask some basic questions at the beginning of the class made it easier for me to ask more difficult ones later in the semester.

In regard to a couple's sexual life, the ability to "ask questions" is even *more* crucial. It has been said that "death" is the least-used word in the English language. While this may be true, it seems that the subject of sex is avoided with equal vigor in many marriages. Yet this can be quite damaging to a couple. If we remain silent about our sexual feelings, uncomfortable or bothersome practices will go uncorrected; and if we don't tell our spouse what we do and do not like, how can we expect him or her to work to change that behavior?

When it comes to human sexuality, ignorance certainly is not bliss. I've counseled couples in their fifties who've missed out on years of sexual pleasure simply because they were afraid to ask each other the most basic questions about sex.

There is no reason why couples can't find answers to their questions. And we don't need to run to secular sources for our information; we can find answers to our sexual queries from numerous Christian professionals. Ed and Gaye Wheat's *Intended for Pleasure*, for example, is an excellent source. This book, and its accompanying tape series, can make a couple feel as though they're getting personal advice from a trusted family physician.

In short, no question pertaining to sex is "dumb." *Failing* to ask a question is the dumb thing to do. Our failure to seek answers to our questions can rob us of the years of pleasure God has given us to enjoy.

Using times of refreshment. A culprit goes unnoticed in many busy homes. It's a thief that can rob a couple of intimate times together. It's name is "being active."

Our culture promotes activity. It's not unusual for both spouses to work full-time, to spend eight to ten hours a week commuting, and to run a "chauffeur service" for the kids. All are part of an active lifestyle.

But due to our hectic schedules, activity easily becomes a substitute for intimacy. And when busy couples finally *do* find time for a sexual encounter, they're disappointed by it. Well who wouldn't be? Who can have a satisfying sex life when constant activity has worn you to a frazzle?

Is there a way to combat this pattern? Is there any way to get that rare creature, "the night alone," off the endangered species list? Like Solomon's bride, why not deliberately schedule a special, refreshing time to energize your romantic relationship? Listen to her words as she suggests a way to keep their sexual life from becoming crowded out by palace activities:

> Come, my beloved, let us go out into the country, let us spend the night in the villages. Let us rise early and go to the vineyards... There I will give you my love (7:10-12).

This wise bride realized that in marriage, a change in setting can light the romantic spark. Just "getting away from it all" can work wonders. In counseling, I often recommend a "second honeymoon" weekend for couples. During a short time away, husbands and wives can escape the pressures of activity and once again find time for one another's embrace.

WE'VE ONLY JUST BEGUN
Ten-year-olds and piano lessons just don't seem to mix. At least that was my impression when I began taking piano lessons years ago. I really *wanted* to learn how to play, but I only had the patience to practice a few minutes at a time. These hurried times of practice did not compensate for the long hours needed to become a truly accomplished pianist.

Couples also need to be patient when it comes to this most intimate of areas. Sexual understanding and enrichment come by means of patient caring. As couples allow themselves the time and permission to ask questions, to experiment with what is pleasing to their spouse, to fill their days with acts of creative caring, and to schedule times of refreshment, a deepening love will blossom between them.

In yet another area of marriage, they will have learned what it means to grow together.

EXERCISES IN GROWING TOGETHER

(1) Some persons are surprised to learn that God heartily endorses the sexual act between husband and wife. With your spouse, discuss how the subject of sex was treated in your home when you were growing up. What attitudes were expressed in your church? How have these attitudes affected your current outlook on sex?

_____

_____

_____

_____

(2) Make up your own "Caring Days" list. Think of ten things you could do to say "I love you" to your spouse _outside_ the bedroom. Commit yourself to doing at least four of these things during the coming week. Revise this list often.

_____

_____

_____

(3) Are you and your spouse able to ask one another questions about your sex life? Think of several "burning questions" you've been longing to ask him or her on this topic—then ask them!

_____

_____

_____

_____

(4) Do you find that outside activities are interfering with times of sexual intimacy? What type of activity is the main culprit? How can you eliminate or minimize its ruinous influence?

_____

_____

_____

_____

(5) Refer to the Personal Marriage Enrichment Program in Chapter Eleven for further helpful information.

NINE

Reaching Out

When was the last time you asked an angel home for dinner? That's right: a real, live angel. Now stop laughing—it *has* happened! The author of the Book of Hebrews mentions what happened to some hospitable folks in his time.

> Let love of the brethren continue. Do not neglect to show hospitality to strangers, for by this some have entertained angels without knowing it (13:1-2).

Unfortunately, few married persons today are in danger of entertaining an angel for the evening. We've become so inhospitable that no self-respecting angel would *want* to come by. But who can blame us? After all, every day we read about the terrible tragedies that befall people who innocently open their doors to strangers. If a home once was a man's castle, today it has become his impregnable fortress.

What am I suggesting? Simply, that hospitality be actively and vigorously practiced in every couple's home. Now hear me clearly. I'm not advocating that you turn your house into a twenty-four-hour hotel for anyone who walks in off the street. But by reaching out to others, I believe your marriage can be wonderfully enriched and strengthened. How? Why? Read on.

TAKING OUR EYES OFF OURSELVES

A couple at our church has a tremendous ministry with younger children. Every summer, you'll find neighborhood children crammed wall to wall in their living room. Carl and Virginia, who are in their seventies, host a Vacation Bible School; for this couple, loving and leading little ones to the Lord has greatly benefited their marriage.

By opening their home to children, these spritely senior citizens discovered an important truth: When we concentrate on the needs of *others*, God honors our hospitality and servanthood by blessing us, the servants. In this case, He renewed Carl and Virginia's love for one another after they had been beset by tragedy.

This couple once had a child of their own. His name was Michael. A beautiful baby, he instantly became the light of their lives. However, complications during his delivery meant that Virginia would never have another child. At the time, that didn't seem to matter. Carl and Virginia were content simply to sit back and watch their son grow.

But that privilege was never to be theirs. Before Michael reached his second birthday, he contracted scarlet fever. In less than forty-eight hours, Carl and Virginia lost the only child they would ever have.

As you can well imagine, they were emotionally shattered. Carl and Virginia never turned their back on God, but they did turn away from other people—particularly friends who had new babies of their own. Their pain was too deep, their identification too great, as they thought about Michael.

A painful silence became part of Carl and Virginia's home. Friends no longer were asked over; invitations they received were gracefully declined. Over time, they even began to turn away from one another, as each was preoccupied with his or her own profound grief.

Then, some forty years after Michael's death, another

little boy showed this couple exactly how much they needed each other—and other people.

Brandon was five years old. He and his parents had just moved into the neighborhood, and, like most boys his age, it didn't take long before he went "discovering." He soon found an immaculately kept garden in his neighbor's yard. So it was that when Carl went back to his garden to do some weeding, he found a little stranger hiding among his two rows of corn.

After that first meeting, Brandon became an "apprentice" gardener, with Carl his reluctant teacher. Even Virginia began to take an interest in Brandon—in spite of herself.

It just so happened that Brandon's parents attended a Bible-believing church in the area that sponsored a Vacation Bible School. Brandon's mother was willing to teach the daily lessons, but she knew her living room would be too small to hold all the children that would attend. Suddenly, she hit on the solution to her dilemma. Right after church, with Brandon in tow, she went over to Carl and Virginia's. She asked them if *they* would be willing to host the VBS. The combination of Brandon's big brown eyes and his mother's fervent appeals won them over; Carl and Virginia agreed to host the meetings.

That was ten years ago. They've hosted VBS classes in their home ever since.

Opening their home to these young children opened a new world for Carl and Virginia. Where once they were concerned only with their grief, they now were busy with the concerns of others. And by reaching out to those around them, they finally were able to cope with the pain of their past. They were freed to devote more time to loving one another and less to grieving over their loss.

Michael's baby shoes and picture still sit in Carl and Virginia's living room. They have not forgotten the pain of losing him. But now Brandon, his younger sister, and many other children, have brought new life to this room. For Carl and Virginia, reaching out to others was a key to marital enrichment. By replacing their grief with the values of Christian hospitality, God blessed them with a renewed and stronger love for each other!

MINISTERING AND BEING MINISTERED TO

Reaching out to others can enrich our marriage in a second way: it allows us to minister, and to be ministered to. Both are important to the process of growing together.

In every church, there always are people who need a special dose of personal concern. Perhaps they are new members of the congregation, a family who has suffered the recent loss of a loved one, or missionaries home on furlough. Having such persons into your home can be a real blessing to them. It communicates love and acceptance. But it also can minister to you and your spouse.

Several months ago, I had the opportunity to talk with a man who had moved to Arizona from the Midwest. In the course of our conversation, he recalled that his parents' home always was opened to others. As a boy, he could remember sitting in G. Campbell Morgan's lap and sharing a bowl of hot cereal with Lewis Sperry Chafer.

At the time, he was oblivious to the fact that one of the finest preachers of his generation and the founder of Dallas Theological Seminary were staying at his house. Still, he *could* appreciate the laughter he shared with these guests, the meals taken together, the rich times of prayer.

Perhaps most importantly, he remembered the love that filled his parents' marriage. To this day, he's convinced that their relationship was strong because they had an active and continuous commitment—a ministry, if you will—to serve others. By giving of themselves, they were blessed in return.

Forgetting our problems in order to serve others, and participating in an active ministry of hospitality, definitely can enhance and enrich our marriage. Why, then, don't more couples reach out to others? Exactly what is holding us back?

WHAT'S HOLDING US BACK?

In *If Those Who Reach Could Touch*, Gail and Gordon MacDonald make an interesting statement:

> We like to reach but not necessarily to touch. We like to be touched, but not necessarily at the expense of reaching. Christ was commanding us to do both (Moody Press, p. 20).

I think that pretty well sums up why many couples don't reach out to others. We don't mind when others touch our lives with their generosity or caring—but we hesitate to reach out to others in return.

Yet if reaching and touching others are at the heart of hospitality, why aren't we practicing these things? I think our failure to incorporate these elements into our marriage can be traced to one problem: taking the first step. We always can think of reasons why we *shouldn't* reach out to others: Oh, the house needs to be cleaned before we can have company over; Oh, anyone we'd invite probably has a hundred invitations already; Oh, the cat may be having kittens that night. There *always* are excuses. But let's be honest for a moment.

For many people, it isn't the inconvenience, but the fear of rejection, that keeps them from reaching out. We hesitate to let people into our home because we fear making ourselves known. Our society relishes privacy. Just look at older homes; the porch is in the front. With modern houses, it's in the back, away from the prying eyes of neighbors.

This hesitancy to reach out to others acts like a surgeon's scalpel in cutting off potential relationships. This should not be true in our marriage. As Paul writes:

> By one Spirit we were all baptized into one body... we were all made to drink of one Spirit. For the body is not one member, but many (1 Cor. 12:13-14).

We behave as though we're "only children," when in

actuality, we have a whole family of brothers and sisters. Proverbs puts it even more plainly:

He who separates himself seeks his own desire, he quarrels against all sound wisdom (18:1).

Thus, given the benefits of hospitality to the process of growing together, why not begin today to open your heart and home to others? If you're a novice at reaching out, here are some basic principles that can help you feel more comfortable as you begin.

THE BASICS OF REACHING OUT

As mentioned earlier, to reach out to others we must first overcome our fear of making the first step. Don't play the games that many couples do. I can't tell you how often I've heard a couple who is starved for fellowship say, "When we stop having arguments, *then* we'll have people over." Other couples play the "possessions" game, saying, "After our house looks as nice as our neighbors', *then* we'll have people over." All such statements are little more than stalling tactics.

One basic element of being hospitable is a willingness to begin *now*. We need to be the kind of people who will reach out "in season and out of season."

There also is a second basic element to having successful times of fellowship—an element the early church recognized.

And day by day continuing with one mind in the temple . . . they were taking their meals together with gladness and sincerity of heart (Acts 2:46).

The members of the early church were never at a loss for good ideas. They realized that having a meal together did more for the body than just provide physical nourishment. It provided a special joy. When believers sat down with one another at a meal their God had provided, they were able to fully enjoy their unity as Christians.

Including food in times of fellowship, then, is a basic part of hospitality. While this may seem a rather simplistic notion, it really can help facilitate times of fellowship. Fred and Lynda understood the truth of this fact after they moved to New England.

This couple had grown up in a church in Texas where dinner parties were a regular part of congregational life. But things were quite different when they arrived in the Boston area. People at their new church were warm and friendly, but nobody ever invited them over for dinner. After several months, they began to wonder whether they would ever find any friends in this church.

Fortunately, the pastor sensed Fred and Lynda's uneasiness over this matter. He explained to them that when people are asked over for dinner in New England, it's usually not just to eat a hurried meal. Rather it indicates that they are being welcomed as close family friends. Soon, the church members got to know Fred and Lynda better, and the long-desired dinner invitations finally were issued.

It's amazing how so simple a thing as breaking bread with someone can demonstrate hospitality and cement friendships. For couples seeking to increase their practice of hospitality, an awareness of this element can enrich their own, and others' lives.

There's one final aspect of hospitality we ought to take to heart; that's realizing that the smallest act of hospitality can have a great impact on other people.

A friend of mine, who's a pastor, has a tremendously busy schedule. Apart from "normal" pastoral functions—Sunday services, weddings, funerals—he also has a counseling ministry and a book-writing career. Recently, he told me that a couple he'd been counseling made a decision for Christ. I asked him what motivated them to do so.

Well, according to my friend, this couple realized how hectic his schedule was. Yet they always noticed that he took time to offer them coffee and to chat before they began their sessions. If such hospitable behavior was a part of the Christian lifestyle, they wanted to know more about Jesus Christ!

When it comes to inviting people into our home, we need to recognize that it doesn't always take a five-course meal to demonstrate hospitality. Just having a couple over for coffee—even when you *haven't* vacuumed in a week—can communicate warmth and acceptance.

IDEAS FOR THE SLIGHTLY MORE AMBITIOUS

As we've already seen, demonstrating hospitality can enrich other people's lives as well as your own marriage. The type of sacrificial love practiced in being hospitable, is the same type of love which forms the cornerstone of a healthy, growing marriage. So if you're committed to reaching out to others (and you should be), and are interested in some additional ways to do so, the following pages are for you!

Have a backyard drive-in theater. During the late spring or summer (this idea doesn't work well in the snow), invite several couples or families to go to the movies. But rather than going to the theater, set up a backyard drive-in!

All this idea takes is a projector or VCR, an extension cord, a sheet hung on the back of the house as a screen, a movie you rent (or which you can check out free at a public library), and an evening without rain. A Disney movie and hot buttered popcorn for the kids can open up doors of friendship.

Invite a couple over for a "regressive" dinner. One couple we know invited us over for a *re*gressive dinner. When we received the invitation, I was certain they had misspelled *pro*gressive. But upon arriving at their apartment, I discovered the spelling *had* been correct! The menu began with dessert in the family room, moved to the main course in the kitchen, and ended up with appetizers out on the porch! This was a novel way to present an old idea, and it made us feel warm and welcomed.

Set up a two-couple ministry project for the holidays. Many of us are richly blessed during the holiday season; this certainly has been true in our household. So as a way of saying "thank You" to our Provider, we try to lend a helping hand to others during the holidays.

This past Christmas, we picked up another couple and their children and headed down to a local mission. Each member of our two families got involved in serving others in the food lines there. Doing a service project with another couple can be a blessing in two ways. The experience itself is a meaningful one; it helps us to remember that all we have comes from the Lord. But we also have found that it raises the level of fellowship between couples by quantum leaps. As couples, we've been drawn into meaningful discussions about what God would have us do with our talents and what it means to be hospitable to others.

Set up a cream puff campout. For those who aren't exactly mountaineers, why not invite several couples along on a cream puff campout? This is a campout that eliminates travel time and frayed nerves, while providing kids and adults with all the enjoyment of experiencing a night in the great outdoors. Have you guessed it by now? That's right: just pitch the tents in your own backyard! You can cook out on the barbeque, play games out back, and then bed down under the stars (all this with the knowledge that the bathroom is only a few feet away!)

Pick-a-culture party. My wife came up with a special way to combine an observation of our church's missions work with an opportunity to reach out to other families. Cindy suggested we should have a "pick-a-culture" party. Our family, along with two others, selected a country we wanted to learn more about. Each family brought books from the library on their country of choice (ones with lots of pictures for the children's sake). We also made decorations indigenous to each country to liven up the room. Finally, we enjoyed a potluck supper of dishes from each culture we had been studying.

The kids loved the books and decorations, and the adults liked sampling the delicacies! We also set aside time to share some specific spiritual facts about our country. What percentage of people there still were without Christ? What struggles were missionaries facing in that particular culture? What could we, as a body of believers, do to support the work of the Gospel in that nation? We closed our time together with prayer for these nations and for the missionaries working in them.

Apart from gaining an enhanced understanding of missions work, each couple felt a sense of being united as members of the body of Christ. It was a perfect example of how hospitality can—and should—be a natural extension of our Christian experience.

These are just a few suggestions you might want to try as you reach out to others. Remember, whether you're sharing a cup of coffee or participating in a backyard campout, you'll be building precious memories and relationships. And don't forget: an important end-product of your efforts in this area will be an improved and enriched relationship with your spouse. As we reach out to others, we can draw closer to our mate. God bless your efforts as you begin the exciting "co-mission" of reaching out to others!

EXERCISES IN GROWING TOGETHER

(1) Apart from the ones discussed in this chapter, can you think of any other reasons why being hospitable can help a couple grow together?

_____

_____

_____

(2) What does the statement, "We like to be touched, but not necessarily at the expense of reaching" mean to you? Do you feel this statement applies to you and your spouse? If so, what can you do to change that situation?

_____

_____

_____

_____

(3) What "small acts of hospitality" have you practiced lately? What ones could you demonstrate in the days ahead? Think particularly how you might apply these ideas to unsaved co-workers, a new couple at church, etc. If necessary, keep a record of your "hospitable" actions to ensure that you're honoring your commitment in this area.

_____

_____

_____

_____

(4) This chapter looked at several ideas for extending creative hospitality to other couples. Come up with a list of at least three other novel ways to reach out to others—then put them to use over the next few weeks!

_____

---

(5) Refer to the Marriage Enrichment Program in Chapter Eleven for further helpful information.

TEN

Growing Together over the Life Cycle

Most of us wouldn't bother to look at a road map if we were just running down to the local store. But very few people would want to begin a long journey, over unfamiliar territory, without some idea of the things they might encounter along the way.

Trying to foresee what lies ahead makes a great deal of sense when it comes to traveling long distances. Yet many couples fail to apply this same logic to their travels through adulthood. One perceptive counselor has remarked in this regard:

> If I were to point out one persistent problem that I see in married couples, it is their utter lack of knowledge of what transpires over the adult life cycle. In some cases, ignorance may be bliss. But when it comes to understanding the impact that can come with changes in the life cycle—ignorance can become a formidable enemy (Michael Burnidge, *The Marital Life Cycle*, unpublished message).

In short, few people understand how the changes that occur during their adult life can disrupt their marriage. They fail to take time to look ahead to the tasks and trials that commonly face their relationship. While an understanding of these factors may not *prevent* trials from happening, it *can* alert couples to crucial events they'll confront in their marriage.

Studying the changes which we undergo during the different phases of our adult life—or, as I prefer to term it, our adult "life cycle"—may seem like a contemporary or avantgarde thing to do. But such a study actually finds its basis in Scripture. In reflecting on the course of life, Solomon noted that there is "An appointed time for everything. And there is a time for every event under heaven" (Ecc. 3:1). In other words, our life consists of identifiable "seasons" which change as we grow older.

Books which examine these "seasons" appear to be extremely popular; life cycle studies have captured shelves in bookstores and space on many bestseller lists. Yet the majority of these books deal only with the impact of the life cycle on *individual* men or women. In the pages that follow, we will focus our attention on how this cycle affects *married couples* in four different areas of their lives. And in so doing, we should be able to discover new and vital ways to grow together.

FOUR MAJOR TASKS FOR GROWING COUPLES

Christian authors also have become interested in exploring the topic of life cycles. In fact, several writers have identified seven (or more) stages they believe individuals pass through during the course of their life and/or marriage. Yet for our purposes, I think it would be more helpful to concentrate on four *tasks* married couples commonly face over their adult life cycle.

What do I mean by tasks? Simply stated, tasks are the challenges that couples need to meet and overcome at critical junctures in their marriage. If these tasks are successfully accomplished, a husband and wife will experience real growth in their relationship. As we look at these tasks, though, we need to keep at least two points in mind.

First, each of these tasks or challenges is more likely to occur when a couple is at a particular age; that is, some tasks will be more applicable to couples in their twenties, others to persons in their thirties, etc. However, this is not to suggest that a task will occur only during one "season" of the life cycle. Mastering a task in one's twenties does not guarantee that a couple will not need to pay attention to it in their forties.

The second point to remember is that some couples will find certain tasks more difficult than others. Often, a couple who breezes through the first few years of marriage will face extremely difficult tasks as they approach mid-life. The tensions that may result from these tasks, then, often depend on circumstances.

With these thoughts in mind, let's now look at the four tasks married couples generally confront.

MAJOR TASKS FOR GROWING COUPLES

Age: Twenties
Task: Authentic Acceptance vs. Unrealistic Expectations

Age: Thirties
Task: Personal Commitment vs. The Quest for Success

Age: Forties
Task: Renewing Commitments vs. Slipping Away

Age: Fifties and Beyond
Task: Intimate Friends vs. Isolation

The first task: Authentic Acceptance vs. Unrealistic Expectations. Most persons who marry in their twenties face the task of dealing with their spouse's—and their own—expectations concerning marriage. Unrealistic expectations in this area can seriously damage a relationship. As David and Vera Mace have observed:

Unfulfilled expectations generate frustration with anger. The higher our expectations, the more numerous our needs, the more often we will find ourselves blocked (*We Can Have Better Marriages If We Really Want Them*, Abingdon Press, p. 87).

Mary always dreamed that when she was married, her husband would shower her with constant attention. In marrying Alan, it seemed her wish had come true. He initiated surprise weekend trips for the two of them, prepared romantic dinners, never forgot a birthday or anniversary. In short, he did everything a husband reasonably could do to show his wife attention. But for Mary, that wasn't enough. If Alan was reading a book, she wanted to know why he wasn't talking with her. If Alan was meeting friends for lunch, she wanted to know why he hadn't asked her to come along too.

Obviously, Mary had come into the marriage with some unrealistic expectations. She thought Alan would want to spend every waking moment with her. When this didn't occur, she began to wonder how she could change his behavior to get him to pay *more* attention to her.

There's an important lesson here. Instead of attempting to change her spouse's behavior to satisfy her own unrealistic expectations, Mary should have concentrated on appreciating and accepting Alan's many positive traits.

This is not to say that couples should avoid discussing their expectations, hopes, and wishes. But married persons in their twenties need to recognize that unrealistic expectations about married life will lead to disappointment. Couples must replace these expectations with an authentic acceptance of their spouse.

The second task: Personal Commitment vs. The Quest for Success. For many couples, the thirties signal a time when a high level of personal accomplishment becomes important. For husbands (and with the increasing number of women in the work force, wives, as well), the thirties can set off a search for success in many areas of life. As Daniel Levinson puts it:

> At the start of this period, a man is on the bottom rung of his ladder and is entering a world in which he is a junior member. His aims are to advance in the enterprise, and to climb the ladder and become a senior member of that world. His sense of well-being during this period depends strongly on his own and other's evaluation of his progress toward these goals (*The Seasons of a Man's Life*, Ballantine Books, p. 73).

Please don't misunderstand me. There's nothing wrong with pursuing goals. But real problems can develop in a marriage when the race for success replaces marital commitment. Dr. Howard Hendricks tells the story of a businessman who had become quite successful, but who sacrificed his relationship with his family in the process. This man sat in Dr. Hendricks' office, shattered and scarred by the breakup of his home. Looking back over the third decade of his life, he said, "I spent years climbing the ladder of success. But when I reached the top, I found out the ladder was leaning against the wrong wall."

After a long and dangerous trip through Oz, little Dorothy learned that there was "no place like home." Unfortunately, many of us stray far from home looking for the wizard named "Success." We can become so engrossed in our search that we ignore our responsibilities to love and care for our spouse. As a result, like the businessman in Dr. Hendricks' story, we can wake up to find we no longer have a home to return to.

The major task for married persons in their thirties, then, is to balance their drives to succeed with a valuable secret found in the Book of Philippians:

> Not that I speak from want; for I have learned to be content
> in whatever circumstances I am. I know how to get along

with humble means, and I also know how to live in prosperity; in any and every circumstance I have learned the *secret* of being filled and going hungry, both of having abundance and suffering need (4:11-12; italics mine).

What's the secret? In a world that tells us to work harder and faster, we are encouraged to slow down and cultivate a contentment that comes from above. We are to pause and meditate on the fact that Jesus already has secured our success—in the areas that *really* matter—with His blood on the cross. We have both *significance* and *security* because of what He's already done for us. Our significance is based on the fact that we have a permanent personal relationship with the living God, one that is not dependent on our performance. We have a security that is freely given, one that does not have to be earned. With this freedom, we can devote more energy to growing together with our spouse, and less to the frantic drive for success.

The third task: Renewing Commitments vs. Slipping Away. Couples in their forties currently are gaining quite a bit of attention. The term "mid-life crisis," for example, has worked its way into our vocabulary largely due to the research being performed on this critical phase of the life cycle.

Now before we take the previous paragraph's assumption for granted—that the forties are a "crisis" time for many persons—let's ask a few questions. First, is a mid-life crisis a genuine condition, or have we simply convinced ourselves it's real? If one were only to look at divorce statistics, it would become apparent that the forties are, in fact, a critical time in many marriages.

Well, if mid-life crisis *is* real, why are we only starting to hear about it today? Why didn't people know about this crisis a century ago? Actually, up until the 1900s, the life expectancy for most American adults was around fifty years of age. Today, the marvels of modern medicine have stretched that average span by over twenty years. As a result, adults are living to face more choices, options, and opportunities than at any other time in history. Sounds pretty terrific, eh?

Think again.

When some men and women reach their forties, they suddenly feel overwhelmed by the magnitude of the decisions they must make—decisions which often will affect them for the rest of their lives. Will I take out another mortgage on the house? How will I finance my kids' college educations? Should I accept this or that job offer?

Faced with such major decisions, the urge to just slip away and "start all over again"—without these crushing responsibilities—seems almost irresistible. Sadly, thousands are doing just that: slipping away from their spouses.

Did you know that most people drown within twenty feet of shore? Think about that for a moment. Couples in their forties are taunted by a society that says, "You've carried the burden long enough. Give up! You can't reach the shore!" Often, such individuals are but a few feet from a phone that can become their lifeline to a concerned friend or counselor.

In his book, *Men in Mid-Life Crisis*, Dr. Jim Conway candidly mentions that other pastures start looking greener once you hit forty. The desire to run after them is overwhelming. But he also points out that God *does* provide a future for persons who remain committed to their spouse:

> Do not let your heart envy sinners, but live in the fear of the Lord always. Surely there is a future, and your hope will not be cut off. Listen my son, and be wise, and direct your heart in the way (Prov. 23:17-19).

Married persons who "give up" in their forties will find out later—to their regret—that they were only a few feet from shore. The God who can cause us to "mount up with wings like eagles," can get us safely there. The task for spouses in their forties is to renew their commitments to one another; they must battle the insidious urge to slip away.

The fourth task: Intimate Friends vs. Isolation. Many married couples in their fifties and sixties tell me they can't believe how quickly the years have flown by. It seems as though only yesterday they were at the altar exchanging wedding vows.

Now, in their fifth and sixth decades of life, they still must complete at least one more task: they need to cement an intimate friendship with one another. If earlier tasks were successfully completed, this final one probably will not be too difficult. But if prior tasks were neglected, couples could be facing a troublesome future.

For most married persons in their fifties and beyond, this period of life is a time of settling down. By now, children usually are out of the house and on their own. Most major career moves will already have taken place. Now, for the first time in years, two people must once again start living as a *couple*.

Studies report that those who have faced and mastered marital tasks during earlier phases of the life cycle will experience an upswing in marital satisfaction. Marriage continues to be a time of growth and discovery for them. Yet other couples, who for years lived with unfulfilled expectations or who grew apart, can face a difficult time in bringing a sense of excitement to their relationship.

Barry and Anne found themselves in this situation. For years, Barry had been too busy with business opportunities to take time for his wife. Now, in his late fifties, Barry began to tire of the corporate game. He suddenly became interested in spending time with his family. This was a wonderful gesture on his part; problem was, it came thirty years too late.

Lacking Barry's companionship, Anne filled the void in her life with her children and friends. When the children were grown, she went back to school for a degree. Now that Barry was ready for family life, Anne was off and running with a new career of her own.

Barry and Anne's story is not an uncommon one. Many couples neglect their marriage for years, then expect it to provide fulfillment when they are older. They seek to reap a harvest of intimate friendship without ever having taken time to sow love's seeds. For Barry and Anne—and for many other couples—isolation, rather than an intimate friendship, characterizes the season of the fifties.

How can couples learn to establish an intimate relationship before it's too late? Consider the example of the ant:

Four things are small on the earth, but they are exceedingly wise: The ants are not a strong folk, but they prepare their food in the summer (Prov. 30:24-25).

The best time to begin storing away positive memories, actions, and experiences, is in the summer of a relationship. Those who go out late in the season and try to gather needed nourishment from their relationship will come back disappointed.

An intimate friendship with a spouse is a gift that can fill up the later years of life; but the absence of a strong relationship will bring a deep sense of isolation.

It is my prayer that every couple who reads this chapter—whatever their season of life—will store up intimacy as they proceed through life. These priceless deposits cannot be purchased in a moment's time. But they can be added in earlier years, to provide warmth and intimacy well into our golden years.

TASK COMPLETION TIPS

We've now seen that couples can grow together by accomplishing certain tasks. Here, then, are two additional tips that should help any couple achieve victory in this crucial area.

The value of mature models. In a couple's journey along the life cycle, they would do well to spend time listening to mature models, to couples who are older than themselves. Why is this so important?

In most churches and social situations, we have few opportunities to mix with persons outside our own age-group. As a result, we miss a good deal of insight and encouragement from those who've already passed through a "season" of the life cycle and mastered its task. Luckily, we've incorporated these "missing models" into the church where I work. In the young couples' class that my wife and I teach, we bring in an "expert" couple at least once a month. We define "expert" couples as those in the church who have been married more than seven years, and who are walking closely with the Lord. The "expert" couple does not prepare a lesson. They just take a few minutes to share something from their life experience. Each couple will share one principle or lesson that God has taught them over the years of their marriage.

Incorporating these "expert" couples into the class has had tremendous results. Each month, another "expert" couple will share something the Lord has taught them. Invariably, a young couple sitting in the class will be struggling with the very same issue in *their* life. Perhaps the problem has to do with being transferred to a strange city, getting along with in-laws, or learning how to cope with a miscarriage. Whatever the subject, our young couples appreciate the counsel of mature models.

Young couples aren't the only ones who've benefited from such contacts, though. Middle-aged couples in our church have commented on how *their* elders' advice has helped them handle certain decisions and problems.

This Sunday, find a couple in your congregation who's been married for a considerably longer time than you and your spouse. Invite them to your home. Spend time listening to how *they've* met the challenges in *their* marriage. By taking time to follow these suggestions, couples can learn how to successfully complete the tasks facing them on the life cycle.

Times of refreshment. Today, the Alaskan Highway is a paved road with miles of breathtaking scenery. But for years, it was little more than a glorified dirt road. As a result, rain or melting snow inevitably created a muddy course through which truckers had to navigate.

A trucker who frequently traversed this muddy road eventually posted a sign at the point where the highway began. People liked it so much that the Forest Service has made it a permanent marker. It's message? "Pick your rut carefully. You'll be in it for the next 2,000 miles!"

Regrettably, many married persons could place this same sign in their homes. Their years together should have been filled with growth and adventure; long-term ruts have developed, instead.

Throughout their adult life cycle, married persons need to experiment with new and different things. Why not try the mountains one year, the beach the next? How about moonlit strolls and early morning swims? Why don't you and your mate teach a Sunday School class, rather than just being "one of the crowd"?

We cannot experience an abundant and challenging marriage if we do away with fun, excitement, new adventure, and romance. A couple will find their journey through life much more enjoyable if they take refreshing breaks along the way.

EXERCISES IN GROWING TOGETHER

(1) Share the best advice an older person or couple ever gave you about marriage. How has that advice affected your relationship with your spouse? Why do you think so few people today listen to the counsel of mature models?

_____

_____

(2) Picture your life as a book, and each decade of your life as a chapter in it. How would you title the chapters of your life you've already lived? What titles would you like to see in the decades to come?

_____

_____

_____

_____

(3) Is "mid-life" crisis something you fear as a couple? Based on the information presented in this book, behavior you've noticed in older couples, and your own experience, what crises do you foresee you and your spouse encountering? What preventative steps can you take to minimize their effects? You might consult with couples your own age to gain their insights on this issue.

_____

_____

_____

_____

(4) In this chapter, we observed the need for couples to establish an intimate friendship early in their marriage. Pretend you've just met your spouse. What would you do to

convince him or her to become your friend?

_____

_____

_____

_____

(5) Refer to the Marriage Enrichment Program in Chapter Eleven for further helpful information.

ELEVEN

A Personal Marriage Enrichment Program

Aristotle is reported to have said, "You stand a far greater chance of hitting a target if you can see it." It is my hope that after ten chapters, couples will be able to score a bull's-eye in the area of marital enrichment.

In looking at ways couples can grow together, we've covered topics from the wedding night to mid-life crisis. But the principles we've examined won't do us any good if they stay on the printed page. We need to move them out of this book and into our marriage! We need a plan to put these principles into action!

I'd like to close this book, therefore, with a sample program that you can adapt or adopt as your own. A number of married couples I've counseled have followed these suggestions and found them extremely helpful. To be really successful, though, an enrichment program needs to have both partners' "fingerprints" on it; so feel free to add your own personal touches to the program that follows.

Before we begin, several points ought to be made. First, couples must commit themselves to working on this program for a specific amount of time *each week*. While you may choose to spend several hours a week together, I recommend that couples spend at least one hour going over each week's exercises. This is a "must" if you are to see sustained growth in your marriage. Decide together whether this time will be in the morning or the evening, whether it will be on a weekday or the weekend. Again, a necessary part of this program, and a prerequisite to growing together, will be setting up a consistent time to meet with one another.

Second, expect Satan to test your commitment to spending time together. But stand firm. Giving up your enrichment time this week can make it that much easier to skip it next week—and the next. You'll find, however, that consistently meeting together is one of the greatest gifts you can give your spouse.

A final point to remember: the time you devote to this program should not become a substitute for personal devotions. Spending time together in God's Word should remain an important part of a couple's week.

Now that we've discussed these points, on to the program!

FIRST MONTH
To erect a sturdy building, you first must lay a strong foundation. This marriage enrichment program begins by focusing on the only real foundation for a couple's later growth—their relationship with the Lord. Here are some suggestions on how to structure each week's enrichment hour in this vital area.

Week One. In this first enrichment hour, discuss chapter two, "How Firm a Foundation?" Go through the chapter one page at a time, pointing out principles to your spouse that you thought were important.

Week Two. During this second hour, focus all your attention on Psalm 119. This psalm can give you a clear picture of the many promises God gives to those who seek Him and spend time in His Word. You may not get through the entire psalm in one hour. But spend time together discussing as many promises as time allows.

Week Three. Prayer also is an important aspect of building a strong spiritual foundation. One of the best ways to learn about prayer is to study the petitions made by individuals in Scripture. During this enrichment hour, examine Daniel's prayer in Daniel 9:1-19. Together, come up with four elements from his prayer that should become a part of your prayers as a married couple.

Week Four. This fourth enrichment time may take a little advanced planning, particularly if you begin this program in a winter month. Instead of having your enrichment time at home, venture out to a place where you can see God's creation. Looking out on God's handiwork, read and discuss Psalm 104 together.

(Week Five). In some months, the day you have chosen for your enrichment hour may provide a fifth opportunity to meet together. Whenever this happens, don't take the night off! Rather, use it to go back over the past month and discuss how things you've learned can make a difference in your relationship.

P.S. Starting with this first month of the enrichment program, put $20 a month into a savings account. We'll talk more about how this money will be spent at the end of the program.

SECOND MONTH

Where do you go once you've begun to establish a strong spiritual foundation? To the first floor, of course! And Genesis 2:24 tells us that "leaving" home is the necessary first step toward "cleaving" to our spouse. During this second month, we'll take time to look at how our family background may be affecting our marriage today.

Week One. Read chapter three, "The Importance of 'Leaving' Home." Discuss those portions of the chapter you found helpful. Honestly evaluate how far you have come in your efforts to "leave" home.

Week Two. Read and discuss each of the home situations pictured in chapter four, " 'Hard-to-Leave' Homes." Are you hesitant to discuss any aspect of your past? Take time to discuss what you can do to resolve past problems with your parents.

Week Three. Several days before your enrichment hour, each of you should make up a short "family tree." Go back at least to your grandparents and share your "roots" with your spouse. This may mean making a call to a family member to get names and information about certain relatives. In discussing your family, identify the traits you feel you share in common with your parents—both positive and negative. How do you feel about this realization?

Week Four. Take this hour to write a letter, or make a cassette tape, to your parents. Tell them things you appreciated about them when you were growing up. At times, we can forget the many things our parents have done for us. Receiving a letter of thanks from their children means a great deal to parents.

THIRD MONTH

Since you have spent the past two months sharing enrichment hours, this next subject should be of particular interest to you. This month, the topic is cleaving to your spouse.

Week One. In chapter five, "Cleaving: A Concept for Courageous Couples," we looked at five characteristics that define cleaving. Go back through the first three principles this week and talk about the place they play in your relationship. If certain aspects of commitment seem to be lacking in your relationship, discuss practical ways you can enrich these areas.

Week Two. This second week, go back through the final two principles on cleaving found in chapter five. Discuss these with one another, along with practical ways to increase your commitment to each other.

Week Three. The night before your enrichment hour, write out a list of "expectations" you had when you entered marriage. Share these with your spouse. Talk about which expectations were realistic, and which were not. Discuss what "dreams" you still hope will become part of your relationship (see chapter ten for more on expectations).

Week Four. You might want to get a baby-sitter for this evening if you have younger children. In this enrichment hour, begin by sharing an intimate dinner together. Then go back through your wedding pictures. Talk about the commitments you made that day. Read your wedding vows if you still have them. By looking at past commitments to one another, use this time to renew your present commitments.

FOURTH MONTH

If you have been meeting faithfully over the last three months, you will already have noticed improvements in your ability to communicate with your spouse. This month, we'll look at the subject of marital communication in greater detail.

Week One. Go back through chapter six, "Communication: Lifeblood of a Relationship." In this enrichment hour, talk specifically about how closely your verbal and nonverbal communication match. You might point out to your spouse things he or she does "nonverbally" to communicate a certain message.

Week Two. During this enrichment hour, plan on having a "mis-communication" night. To do this, read the section on "Seven Great Ways to Kill Communication." Then take turns actually trying out some of these "communication killers." Be deliberately vague, talk to one another from across the room, etc. Discuss what it was like to experience these misdirected communication attempts. Understanding what it's like to receive such messages can help keep your communication clear and unobstructed. Remember, you should use these communication killers only during this *one* night! Don't make them a habit!

Week Three. Use a tape recorder this week to learn more about the sound of your own voice. Tape a "normal" conversation with your spouse, then "play act" an argument (try to be realistic without opening up real wounds!). Listen closely to the tone of your voice; what does it tell you about the way you come across in a conversation?

Week Four. Go through the "Communication Creed" found at the end of chapter six. How well do you practice these points?

FIFTH MONTH

By now, if you've been practicing the principles covered in earlier enrichment hours, you should be able to minimize conflict in your marriage. Still, there's always *more* we can learn about this important topic.

Week One. Read the portion of chapter seven, "Conquering Conflict," that deals with the function of friction in a married couple's life. Have you ever tried to produce changes in your marriage through conflict?

Week Two. Six guidelines were presented in this same chapter to prepare couples to deal with disagreements. During this enrichment hour, discuss the first three and how they can be applied to your relationship.

Week Three. Discuss the final three guidelines on handling conflict in the home this week. Take particular note of what "level" of conflict you frequently reach. Discuss what you could do to keep arguments on the "ground floor" in your marriage.

Week Four. In this enrichment hour, you will need a concordance to find Scripture verses. Together as a couple, make a topical study of all the verses in Proverbs that mention "anger," the "wise man," and the "fool." How can these verses be applied to dealing with marital disagreements?

SIXTH MONTH

As we noted in chapter eight, "Drink Deeply, O Lovers," sex sometimes can be an embarrassing topic to discuss. But in an enriched marriage, it's an area we cannot afford to ignore.

Week One. Read over chapter eight. Discuss the chart that

pictures the various "layers of life" which can affect our sexual lives. Which "layer" drains away the most sexual energy for you? Discuss how you can triumph over this area.

Week Two. Understanding how we differ physically and emotionally from our spouse can help improve a couple's sexual life. I recommend Gary Smalley's companion volumes, *If He Only Knew,* and *For Better or For Best* to most couples I counsel. While they don't deal specifically with sex, they do an excellent job of pointing out the different ways husbands and wives respond to each other. Reading and discussing his chapters on "differences" can help keep each "layer of life" uncluttered.

Week Three. Remember that God, Himself, set aside an entire Old Testament book to talk about marital love. Take time to read the Song of Solomon together, and learn from the beautiful picture of love it presents.

Week Four. Before you meet together for this night's enrichment hour, write out the answers to two questions. "What does my spouse do that pleases me sexually?" and "Sex would be even more fulfilling for me if . . . . " Be sensitive, but courageous, as you discuss these questions with your spouse.

P.S. Are you remembering to put aside $20 each month?

SEVENTH MONTH

If you have spent the past six months in weekly enrichment times, you're almost ready to conduct your own marriage seminars! To do so, though, you'd have to know how to reach out to other people. So take a month to focus on developing hospitality as a married couple.

Week One. Go back through chapter nine, "Reaching Out." This first week, draw up a list of the things you think hold you and your spouse back from sharing with others. This exercise can help you determine the fears that keep you from reaching out to others. Discuss how you can overcome these fears.

Week Two. Plan to spend a creative evening with another married couple. Decide on the menu and what activities will take place. Then close your enrichment hour by taking the first step: call your prospective guests with an invitation! Be sure to give this couple at least a week's notice.

Week Three. Spend this time by praying for the friends you've invited over. Praying ahead of time for a meaningful evening can help you to be sensitive to your guests when they're in your home.

Week Four. After your evening of creative hospitality, talk about your expectations and reactions. Was any aspect of being a host and hostess uncomfortable? What was encouraging?

P.S. Drop me a note if you come up with a creative idea for bringing people together for fellowship or outreach. I'm always looking for new ideas to share with others; I'd love to hear what you come up with. Write: Dr. John Trent, Scottsdale Bible Church, 7601 E. Shea Blvd., Scottsdale, AZ 85260. Thanks!

EIGHTH MONTH

Expect great things to continue over each season of life as you increase your commitment to each other. This month's topic focuses on the challenges couples can face as they go through the adult life cycle.

Week One. Read over chapter ten, "Growing Together Over the Life Cycle." During this first week, look at the season of the "twenties" and the task involved for married persons in this age-bracket. What does "authentically accepting" your spouse mean to you? If you are past your twenties, consider how you dealt, or are dealing, with this task.

Week Two. During this week, discuss the season of the "thirties" and its particular task. How are you reacting to our society's pressure to succeed? If you aren't yet thirty, discuss how you will handle this task in the future; if you are in this age-group, follow the directions for week one.

Week Three. During this third week, look at the season of the "forties." You might want to read Jim Conway's book, *Men in Mid-Life Crisis* before you discuss the crises that can occur at this age. How can you successfully handle the responsibilities of this time? Even if you are years away from your forties, this still can be a valuable time of discussion. Being forewarned can make you forearmed to changes during this period.

Week Four. Plan to spend this last enrichment time with an older couple. In your home, or at a restaurant, ask them to recount and reflect on their years of marriage. You'll learn a great deal and it will be a blessing to them, as well.

NINTH MONTH

This particular marriage enrichment program is about to come to a close. You may not realize it, but over the eight months of this program, you and your spouse met together to enrich your marriage over *thirty* times! But there still is one important area you must examine. Basically, you need to evaluate the extent to which you and your spouse have grown together over this time. If you try to short-cut this evaluation process, you'll miss out on two things. First, you'll be unaware of how much growth actually has taken place. Second, you won't know which areas of your marriage still need strengthening in the months to come.

Remember the $20 that you've been putting away each month? Now is the time to raid the savings account, send the kids over to your parents, and head for the hills—or at least a nearby hotel. Taking a weekend trip can be a perfect way to get away from the phone and to start evaluating your marriage.

Before you leave for your weekend, however, think through the past eight months. List ten aspects of your marriage you believe have been improved through enrichment times. Once you're on your weekend trip, share these thoughts with your spouse. After you have done this, discuss areas in your marriage you feel still need work.

These concerns can form the basis for your *next* marriage enrichment program. Take time to plan out another eight-month program of marital growth. You can keep the same format and cover the topics in this program in greater depth. Or, you can include new topics like family finances, Bible study methods, or dealing with stress. If you find it difficult to come up with new topics, check with your pastor for ideas.

After you've spent the day talking about all God has accomplished in your marriage through this enrichment program, take the evening off. Enjoy a special dinner together; create an evening of romance.

THE CHALLENGE

If it seems as though we've only begun to scratch the surface on ways to enrich your marriage, you're right! And isn't that wonderful? If growing together were a process that could be accomplished over the course of a few days, marriage would be a rather shallow enterprise. But God, in His wisdom, has provided us with a relationship that can offer years of excitement, challenge, and fulfillment.

An old proverb states, "A journey of a thousand miles begins with a single step." Some persons who've read this book already have started taking steps toward enriching their marriage. Others may just be beginning. Wherever you are in this journey, I pray that the roads you travel will enhance and improve your marriage. My wish is that the program presented in this book will aid you in growing together through each season of life.